MANAGEMENT:

PROCESSES AND PARADIGMS

for the

Twenty-First Century

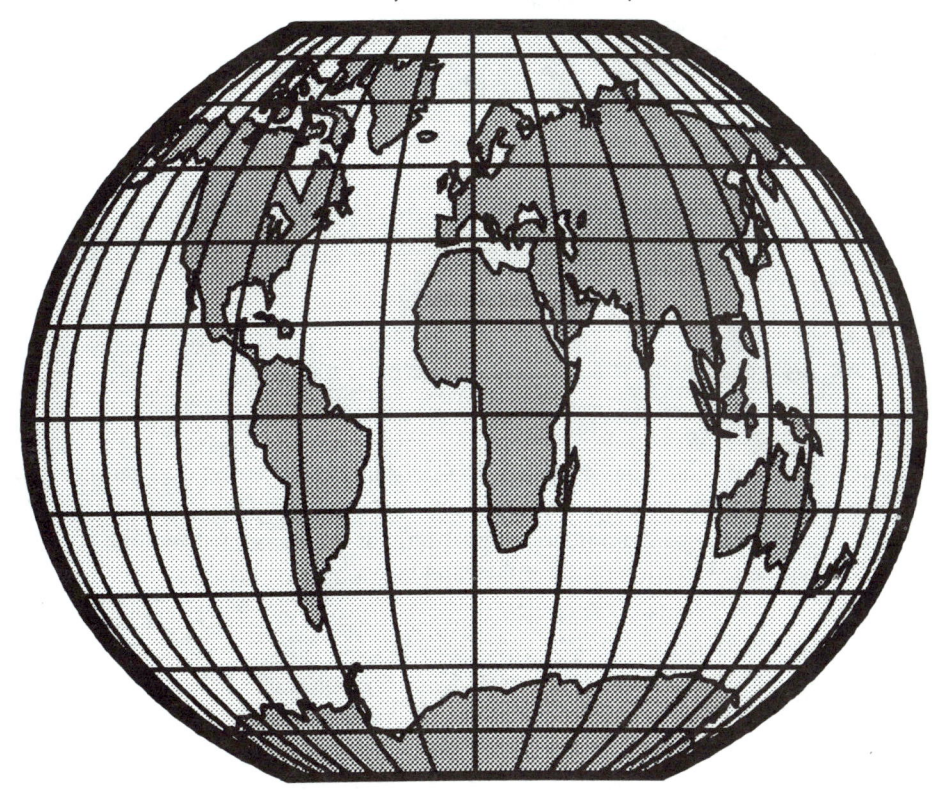

Dr. Benjamin F. Findley, Jr., RFC

President
Professional Management Resources Company
Pensacola, Florida

Copyright © 1999 by Benjamin F. Findley, Jr.

Professional Management Resources Co.
5927 Hermitage Drive
Pensacola, FL 32504-7932

Cover Design and Drawing by Karolyn Annette Findley

All rights reserved. No part of this publication may be reproduced, stored in a retrieval system, or transmitted in any form or by any means, electronic, mechanical, photocopy, recording, or otherwise, without the prior written permission of the author and the publisher, Professional Management Resources Company.

Printed in the United States of America

ISBN 0-96-18129-3-1

FOREWORD

We are experiencing a tremendously exciting and challenging period for the understanding and practice of the management process. Now, as never before, there is a growing recognition of the value of effective management and leadership of our resources, especially the human resource. Our dynamic industrialized work force with its high level of education, its scientific and technological advancement, and its abundance of information, brings the challenges of resolving organizational problems by consensus and collaborative, win-win approaches. Whether our organization is of a business, government, school, military, or not-for-profit nature, we realize the critical importance of planning, organizing, coordinating, directing, and controlling our resources through application of tested concepts and principles and contemporary tools and techniques to get our results.

This book is a blend of proven principles, distinct processes, practical paradigms, and useful techniques to add to your base of management knowledge and to improve your managerial skills. It is written in an easy-to-read style that is broad enough in scope to permit its application to a number of organizations and situations. Yet is has sufficient depth in the basic functions and techniques of management and the processes of motivation, leadership, problem solving, decision making, team building, and communication.

Dr. Findley's book is a useful and fundamental approach to organizational management and I commend it to you as a conceptually sound, empirically-based, and practically-oriented resource for your use in the Twenty-First Century.

John A. Kline

Dr. John A. Kline, Senior Executive Service
Provost
Air University
Maxwell Air Force Base, Alabama

AUTHOR PROFILE

DR. BENJAMIN F. FINDLEY, JR., RFC, is President of Professional Management Resources Company, a private Florida firm specializing in offering management training seminars for managers and employees, management resource books, and financial consulting services. He has over 25 years of experience as an industrial personnel director for Pfizer Pharmaceutical Company in New York City and with Abbott Laboratories in Austin, Texas, as a U.S. Air Force Colonel in Air University's Provost Office, international military-political affairs, and personnel, and in higher education as dean, professor, and administrator for colleges and universities. His doctorate is in business/teaching from the University of Northern Colorado, his master's is in industrial relations and his bachelor's is in business, both from West Virginia University. He has completed post-doctorate and advanced management study at the University of Texas in Austin, the Air Force Institute of Technology, and the University of California at Davis.

Dr. Findley is the author of several books and articles, as well as a U.S. Air Force required course in principles of supervision in CD-ROM format. He has presented numerous leadership, financial management and investing, human resources, organizational and personal management training workshops. He is certified as a Registered Financial Consultant (RFC) with the International Association of Registered Financial Consultants and is a certified U.S. Small Business Administration Consultant.

For ten years, Ben has served Pensacola Junior College, Florida as Dean, School of Business, Human Resources Director, and Risk Management & Legal Affairs Director. Since 1994, he has served as an adjunct graduate professor of management for the University of Arkansas at the Fort Walton Beach, FL Center, where he teaches strategic management, financial management, and human resources management in their master's degree program. He has also served as Dean of the College of Business and Professor of Management at the University of Sarasota in Florida.

Ben is Past Chapter President for the Florida College and University Personnel Association and a recipient of their "Outstanding Human Resource Practitioner Award" in 1995. He is also past Chairman of the Florida Community Colleges Human Resources Council and past Chairman of the Board for the Foundation for Excellence in Education, Escambia County School District. Presently, he serves as President of the Public Risk Management Association, North Florida and Alabama Chapter. He is listed in Who's Who in American Education, Who's Who in the South and Southwest, Personalities of America, Who's Who in Organizational Development, and Who's Who in Training and Development.

His broad management background is represented by his diverse experiences. In 1997, he was appointed representative to the Florida State Committee for Employer Support of the Guard and Reserve. He serves as the U.S. Air Force Reserve's representative on the Air War College Foundation Board of Directors and their Financial Planning Committee. He was awarded the U.S. Air Force Academy's outstanding counselor award for Academy liaison officers in Region II, where he serves as Deputy Commander for Northwest Florida and Alabama. Dr. Findley has served on a Southern Association of Colleges and Schools (SACS) Evaluation Team and as a NCAA Football Official for seven years with the Southwest Football Officials Association. Ben resides in Pensacola, Florida with his wife Karen, two daughters Karolyn and Susan, and dog Ollie.

1998

Table of Contents

FOREWORD	iii
AUTHOR PROFILE	iv
EXHIBITS	xv
DEDICATION	xvii

PART I. FUNDAMENTALS OF MANAGING   1

    A. The Nature of Management and Supervision   1

       1. Management, Supervision,
          and Leadership Concepts   1
       2. Managerial Functions and Roles   3
          a. Planning
             1. Benchmarking
          b. Organizing
          c. Directing
          d. Coordinating
          e. Controlling
       3. Basic Principles, Skills, and Behaviors For
          Successful Management   5
          a. Fayol's Principles
          b. Management By Exception Principle
          c. Objectivity Principle
          d. Adaptability Principle
          e. Administrative-Conceptual, Human,
             and Technical Skills

    B. Group Dynamics, Organizing, and
       Team Building   10

1. Effective Group Criteria, Conditions,
   and Behaviors   10
   a. Elements of Effectiveness
   b. Restructuring
   c. Empowerment and Self-Managed Teams
   d. Diversity
      1. Bases for Diversity
      2. Barriers in Dealing
         With Diversity
2. Group Development and
   Organizational Politics   18
   a. Stages of Group Development
   b. Characteristics of a
      High-Performing Team
   c. Synergy
   d. Group Cohesiveness
   e. Organizational Politics
      1. Definition and Concept
      2. Strategies for Increasing
         Power
3. Teams, Teamwork, and Consensus   23
   a. Team Roles
   b. Consensus Concept
   c. Consensus Definition
   d. Creating a Climate for Consensus
   e. Types of Team/Group Behaviors
      1. Self-Oriented Behaviors
      2. Assertive Behavior

C. Managing Change and Interpersonal Relations   30

1. Change: Organizational and
   Individual Perspectives   30
   a. Change Process
   b. Responses to Change
   c. Change Strategies
   d. A Learning Organization

e. Organizational Development (OD)
   1. OD Objectives
   2. OD Characteristics
f. Key Equal Employment Opportunity Legislation
2. The Coaching Role for Managers　　36
   a. Constructive Confrontation
   b. Hidden Agendas
   c. Focus on Issues, Not Blame
   d. Focus on Mutual Benefits, Not Win-Lose
   e. Time Delay Value
3. The Counseling Role for Managers　　39
   a. The Performance Counseling Concept
   b. Specific Signs of a Troubled Worker
   c. Clarification of Performance Standards
   d. Counseling vs. Disciplinary Action
   e. Basic Counseling Function
   f. Guidelines for Worker Counseling
4. Conflict Resolution　　43
   a. Dealing With Opposition To Your Ideas
   b. Interpersonal Conflict Resolution Styles
   c. Situational Considerations
   d. Collaboration Skills
   e. Resolution Hints
   f. Techniques for Dealing With Specific Problem People
   g. Consensus and Win-Win

PART II. THE PROCESS OF EFFECTIVE COMMUNICATION　　52

A. The Communication Process　　52

   1. Purpose
   2. Elements
   3. Feedback
   4. Common Barriers

B. Oral and Written Communication   56
1. Formal and Informal Channels
2. The Grapevine
3. Selective Perception
4. Status Differences
5. Logical Reasoning Fallacies That Hinder Communication

C. Strategies for Successful Communication   62
1. Understand Nonverbal Messages
2. Develop Listening Skills
3. Utilize Feedback and Follow Up
4. Guidelines for Effective Communication
5. Key Negotiation Strategies
6. Openness and Trust Model: Johari Window

D. Technological Factors in Communication   70
1. The Internet
2. Cyberspace Law Considerations
   a. Computer Crime
   b. Electronic-Mail
   c. Cyberstalking

PART III. THE PROCESS OF PLANNING EFFECTIVE GOALS AND OBJECTIVES   78

A. Importance of Planning   78

B. Planning Steps   78

C. Types of Plans   79

D. The Goal and Objective Setting Process   80
1. Goals versus Objectives
2. Purposes of Objectives
3. The MBO Process

E. Characteristics of Practical Objectives   82

F. Criteria for Verifiable Objectives 82

G. Relevant Considerations for Planning and Setting
   Objectives 84
   1. Mission and Vision Statements
   2. Priorities
   3. SWOT Analysis
      a. Technique
      b. Typical SWOT Questions
   4. Employee Involvement and Empowerment
   5. Assumptions and Limitations

H. The Delegation of Authority Process 88

   1. Delegation Philosophy and Attitude
   2. Steps in the Delegation Process
   3. Key Considerations in Successful Delegation
      a. Objective Specificity
      b. Objective Difficulty
      c. Feedback
      d. Participation
   4. Overcoming Obstacles to Effective Delegation
      a. Acceptance
      b. Common Barriers
   5. Checklist for Effective Delegation

PART IV. THE MOTIVATION PROCESS
   AND HUMAN BEHAVIOR 94

A. The Complex Motivation Process 94
   1. The Concept
   2. Internal Versus External Influences on Behavior
   3. Attitudes and Job Satisfaction
   4. The Hawthorne Effect
   5. Behavior Modification and Reinforcement

B. The Role of Values in Explaining and

Predicting Behavior 99
    1. Definition of Values
    2. Allport's Types of Values
    3. Dominant Values in Today's Work Force
    4. A Core Values Model
    5. Values in Successful Organizations
    6. Total Quality Management (TQM)
        a. Deming's 14 TQM Points
        b. TQM Elements

C. Needs and Their Implications for Performance   108
    1. Needs Assessment Exercise
    2. Maslow's Need Hierarchy
    3. Alderfer's ERG Model
    4. McClelland's Three-Needs
    5. Useful Conclusions About Needs

D. Motivation Models   115
    1. McGregor's Theory X and Theory Y
    2. Herzberg's Motivators and Hygiene Factors
    3. The Vroom and Porter-Lawler Expectancy Models
    4. Hackman and Oldham's Job Characteristics Model
    5. Assessing a Job's Motivating Potential
    6. Useful Conclusions about Motivation

E. Integrating the Motivational Concepts for
   Practical Implications   122
    1. Blending Behavior, Values, Needs, and Motivation
    2. Positive Climate Guidelines
    3. Predicting Performance

PART V.   LEADERSHIP ISSUES AND MODELS   125

A. The Nature of Leadership   125
    1. Leadership Issues
    2. Cultural Variables
    3. Characteristics of Effective Followers
    4. Power

B. The Trait Model 127

C. Leader Behavior Models 127
1. Blake and Mouton's Managerial Grid
2. Tannenbaum and Schmidt's Continuum
3. Ohio State University Studies
4. Likert's University of Michigan Studies

D. Situational Models 130
1. Fiedler's Contingency Model
2. House's Path-Goal Model
3. Hersey-Blanchard's Life Cycle Model

E. Transformational Leadership 138
1. Concept and Definition
2. Characteristics of Transformational Leaders
3. Productivity and Satisfaction Relationship

F. Leadership Conclusions 139

PART VI. CONTROLLING AND MANAGING TIME 141

A. Basic Planning and Time Management 141
1. Inventory of Personal Time Utilization
2. Time Use Quiz
3. Time Use Quiz Optimal Answers
4. Time Management Concepts
5. Importance and Time Allocation

B. Time Management Philosophy 147
1. Facts, Assumptions, and Attitude
2. Self-Management System
   a. Know Goals, Objectives, and Priorities
   b. Useful Time Management Tools
3. Guidelines for Time Success
   a. Top 10 Time Management Guidelines

C. Time Management Problems and Suggestions   150
 1. Specific Problems and Solutions
 2. Managing Interruptions
 3. General Time Saving Techniques
 4. A Work Priority System

PART VII. DECISION MAKING AND CREATIVE
 PROBLEM SOLVING   159

A. Decision Making Versus Creative
 Problem Solving   159

B. The Decision Making-Problem Solving Process   160
 1. Overview
 2. The Process

C. Selected Tools and Techniques   163
 1. Brainstorming
 2. Cause and Effect Diagrams
 3. Pareto Analysis
 4. Nominal Group Technique
 5. Delphi Technique
 6. Other Techniques
  a. Cost-Benefit Analysis
  b. Marginal Analysis
  c. Myers-Briggs Type Indicator
  d. Program Evaluation and Review Technique (PERT)
  e. Breakeven Point Analysis

D. Concepts and Strategies of Scientific
 Problem Solving   169
 1. Incomplete Information Concept
 2. Satisficing Concept
 3. Strategies
 4. Suboptimization

E. Suggested Problem Solving and
   Decision Making Guidelines   172
   1. Guidelines
   2. Group Behaviors
   3. Ethical Considerations
      a. Definitions
      b. Characteristics of Moral Standards
      c. Fostering Work Ethics

BIBLIOGRAPHY   177

INDEX   183

ORDER FORM   195

LIST OF EXHIBITS

EXHIBIT	EXHIBIT NO.	PAGE
Fayol's 14 Principles	1	5
Findley's Effectiveness Elements	2	11
Dealing With Problem People	3	48
SWOT Analysis	4	85
Dominant Values in Today's Work Force	5	100
Air Force Core Values	6	101
Deming's 14 TQM Points	7	107
Needs Assessment Exercise	8	108
Herzberg's Motivators & Hygienes	9	116
Hackman & Oldham's Job Model	10	120

LIST OF EXHIBITS, Continued

EXHIBIT	EXHIBIT NO.	PAGE
Fiedler's Contingency Model	11	132
Hersey-Blanchard's Model	12	137
Transformational Leaders' Characteristics	13	138
Time Use Quiz	14	142
Work Priority System	15	157
Decision Making Problem Solving Process	16	160

This book is DEDICATED:

IN HONOR OF:

Karen Ann Findley

Susan Elizabeth Findley

Karolyn Annette Findley

IN MEMORY OF:

Benjamin J. Findley, Sr.

Georgia Lee Utterback Findley

Margaret Frances Davis Utterback McCann

Virgil Chester McCann

Hial James Utterback

Everett Eldon Findley, Sr.

J. Pearl Bartlett Findley

MANAGEMENT: PROCESSES AND PARADIGMS
by Dr. Benjamin F. Findley, Jr.

This book examines the fundamental principles, concepts, models, and processes of effective management. All levels of the management team should have an understanding of these basic elements of the management process. In particular, supervisors, as the first-line managers who are directly responsible for overseeing and directing the workers in accomplishing activities to meet organizational goals, must have in-depth knowledge and practical applications of them. Because they are daily in immediate and direct contact with the workers, supervisory managers are an essential leadership and managerial link between and among others managers and the workers. Certainly, all managers significantly contribute to an organization's purpose by ensuring that work tasks and goals are met and processes applied.

FUNDAMENTALS OF MANAGING

The Nature of Management and Supervision

This chapter examines the management, supervision, and leadership concepts, fundamental managerial functions and roles, and basic principles, skills, and behaviors for achieving success in management processes.

Management, Supervision, and Leadership Concepts

Initially, it is important to have an understanding of the definitions and concepts of management, supervision, and leadership, so managers can know what they are to do in performing their roles and functions. **"Management"** is defined as a process of obtaining, deploying, and utilizing a variety of essential resources to accomplish an organization's mission, goals and objectives. An organization's human resource is a very important resource and managers, especially supervisors as first-line managers, spend a large amount of time and effort performing the five functions of planning, organizing, directing, controlling, and coordinating the human resource to achieve stated goals and objectives. All managers, including supervisory managers, perform the identical five functions, but the mix of time devoted to the functions varies by managerial level. Managers, and the work they do, differ mainly according to their level in the organizational hierarchy and the commensurate, assigned authority and responsibility. Managers at different levels spend different amounts of time performing the five functions. At the top of an organization are executive mangers, who have responsibility and authority to manage a group of other managers. They spend considerable time planning and establish broad plans, goals, and general policies, while motivating, organizing, directing, and controlling managers who report to them. Middle managers plan, organize, initiate, implement, and control programs that are intended to carry out the broader goals and policies set by executive managers. Middle managers coordinate, organize, direct, motivate and control the supervisors and other managers who report to them. Supervisors are first-level operating managers who usually report to middle managers and have the responsibility of getting hands-on employees to accomplish tasks to directly carry out the plans, policies, and procedures set by executive and middle-level managers.

Supervisory managers plan, organize, motivate, direct, and control the work of non-managerial employees at the operational level of the organization. Thus, **"supervision"** is defined as a process of primarily directing, controlling, coordinating and motivating the human resource, as well as other operational resources, for the purpose of accomplishing organizational missions, goals, and objectives. The Taft-Hartley Act specifically defines a "supervisor" as a person who has the formal authority to hire, transfer, suspend, layoff, recall, promote, discharge, assign, reward, or discipline other employees and uses independent judgment. Other Federal legislation, the Fair Labor Standards Act for example, considers employees to be supervisors if they direct the work of two or more employees, spend no more than 20 percent of their time performing the same kind of work that their employees do, and if they are paid a salary with no compensation for overtime.

"Leadership" is the process of guiding and directing the behavior of others toward the accomplishment of goals and objectives. Leadership is not the same as management. Although some managers are leaders and some leaders are managers, leadership and management are not the same process. Leadership is a subset of management that focuses on inspiring people and raising human potential. Management is broader in scope, deals with all five functions, and focuses on behavioral and non-behavioral issues, resources, and functions, while leadership focuses mainly on behavioral issues, influencing the human resource, and related functions. Managers should recognize over the long run that although all managers are not necessarily leaders, the most effective managers are leaders that effectively deal with the human resource.

Managerial Functions and Roles

In carrying out their responsibilities, managers perform five basic management functions:

> Planning: Setting intermediate, short-term, and long-term goals and objectives in view of the long-term vision and mission; establishing plans, policies, procedures, practices, and rules

> Organizing: Arranging jobs, tasks, and resources to be completed and utilized in such a way as to make them more effective; delegation of authority and responsibility

> Directing: Giving job instructions and telling others what and sometimes how to accomplish a task or job; uses communication, motivation, leadership, decision making, and time management processes

> Controlling: Regulating the processes, their costs, and the human resources who carry them out

<u>Coordinating:</u> Ensuring that all parts of the organization work together in harmony; integrating all activities, objectives, processes, and resources in support of the total organizational system

Supervisors, as first-level managers, generally spend the most time with (in priority order) the directing, controlling, and coordinating functions. Usually, supervisors spend less time planning, relative to all the five functions. Executive managers, however, spend most time planning and coordinating and less time directing, while middle managers spend the most time directing and planning, in priority order.

All managers are expected to learn and practice specific roles in order to successfully execute their duties. The precise role of each manager depends on his or her understanding of the job responsibilities and authorities, as well as the paradigms, pressures, rewards, sanctions, and guidelines from inside the organization, as well as external factors. The subordinates, peers, friends, family, and superiors of managers help shape and define the kind of roles the manager must perform. As a manager you will find yourself having a significantly different set of relationships. Your relationship with former coworkers and employees will be redefined. You may be perceived as having "sold out" to the bosses and it may be difficult to give orders to former peers, especially those who were close friends. You may feel caught in the middle between your employees and higher management. You may even be tested by your former peers. It is natural during this transition phase for managers to develop excessive sensitivity toward employee behaviors and comments. As a manager, you must avoid this hypersensitivity, be objective, and accept your managerial role as not making your personal worth any better than your former peers because of your position, but as one with different organizational responsibilities. To achieve an effective transition, you must treat each of your employees fairly and provide them with adequate training, direction, and a decent working environment. You must develop a management attitude and identify in a positive manner with the goals and objectives of your organization and willingly follow its policies and procedures, for the benefit of all employees and the organization. Effective managers balance the application of their skills between the work to be done and a concern for the people who perform this work.

Planning and Benchmarking

An important part of planning is understanding what your top competitors are accomplishing, what their plans and goals are, and what their practices are for getting the best results, so your organization can focus on worthwhile areas, conserve resources, and achieve optimal outcomes. Benchmarking is a process of learning how to achieve the very best results by analyzing the plans, goals, and practices in various functional areas of an organization's top competitors. The following *Benchmarking guidelines* are offered for organizations:

1). **Focus on a specific problem, process, or practice.**

2). **Organize and empower an interdisciplinary team of workers** in your organization who will actually be responsible for objectively planning and implementing identified changes in your organization.

3). **Share information from your organization** with the benchmark organization whom you are studying, to establish a mutually-beneficial long-term (win-win) relationship.

4). **Do not search for proprietary and new product or process information**, since you cannot afford to jeopardize relationships and risk litigation.

5). **Keep all information discovered confidential.**

Basic Principles, Skills, and Behaviors for Successful Management

Fayol's Principles: EXHIBIT # 1

Management is recognized as a separate process consisting of distinct functions and based upon certain principles. In 1916, Henri Fayol, a chief executive of a French mining company, advanced 14 generally accepted principles of management which provide basic guidelines for carrying out the management process. The following summarized principles of management are important for managerial decisions and actions:

1. **DIVISION OF WORK/SPECIALIZATION.** Work should be divided into parts so that separate individuals will specialize in work tasks. In operating an office, for example, one person will file correspondence, another will order supplies, and another will answer customer complaints. Areas of specialization should be chosen, so that energies and efforts can be concentrated to gather knowledge, skills, and proficiencies in order to become masters of their fields.

2. **AUTHORITY & RESPONSIBILITY.** Managers must have the right (authority) to give orders and instructions, but they must also accept responsibility for getting the work done correctly. Authority must be commensurate with delegated responsibility.

3. **UNITY OF COMMAND.** Every individual should have only one supervisor. When an employee reports to more than one supervisor, confusion, conflict, and ineffectiveness usually result. Span of control recognizes that there is a limit to the number of individuals any one supervisor can manage effectively. Usually, the higher level manager supervises a smaller number of subordinates. A supervisor may be unable to exercise authority effectively if the number of subordinates is too large. A. V. Graicunas developed the following formula to compute the factors that impact an individual's **span of control**:

$$C = n \left(\frac{2^n}{2} + n - 1 \right)$$

"C" is the total potential subordinate contacts (supervisory span of control) and "n" is the number of subordinates. Note by the formula that 5 subordinates means 100 potential contacts or relationships, while 7 subordinates means 490 possible relationships.

4. **UNITY OF DIRECTION.** Every organization should have only one overall mission, master plan, and one set of goals to follow.

5. **EMPHASIS ON THE TOTAL SYSTEM.** All employees, especially managers and supervisors, must place their interests and goals second to those of the total organization. There must be *subordination of individual interests*. Managers and those in authority must not go their own way because in the long run the total organization will suffer. If the total system is not perpetuated, then the subsystems will not exist and individuals will not exist within the organization.

6. **CHAIN OF COMMAND.** Orders and instructions should flow down a scalar chain from the highest manager to the lowest manager. Likewise, formal communications and complaints should move upward within the channel. Problems seem to occur when individuals are bypassed within the channel for communications, complaints, and instructions. Practice has shown that it is effective to also encourage the exchange of work information laterally between departments, while maintaining the priority of the chain of command.

7. **DISCIPLINE.** Managers, supervisors in particular, are responsible for instilling and extracting discipline and building morale among members of their work force. If employees are expected to be loyal, cooperative, and meet established standards of job performance, then supervisors should meet these expectations in return.

8. **REMUNERATION.** Pay and rewards should reflect each individual's efforts and, most importantly, each person's contribution to the organization's goals. Each employee should be paid according to their individual worth rather than the whim of a manager.

9. **ORDER.** There should be order for all organizational processes and activities. Routine procedures should be specified for everything to avoid waste and minimize effort for efficiency. Managers should be systematic, methodical, and orderly in carrying out their responsibilities.

10. **EQUITY.** All employees should be treated fairly and equally. Managers should not give special consideration to one employee and not another. Dissatisfaction, conflict, and ineffectiveness result when equity does not exist.

11. **INITIATIVE.** Managers should encourage initiative among employees. Managers must recognize the organizational benefit of employee initiative and worker job satisfaction, even if they must sacrifice their personal vanity and sense of satisfaction.

12. **CENTRALIZATION.** The optimum degree of centralized and/or decentralized decision making at a single point in the organization depends on that particular organization's goals and the personal character of the manager, his moral worth, on the reliability of subordinates, and the condition of the business.

13. **STABILITY OF TENURE.** Time is required for an employee to get used to new work and succeed in doing well, assuming that he or she possesses the requisite abilities. If, when he or she has gotten used to it, or before then, he or she is removed, he or she will not have had time to render worthwhile service.

14. **ESPRIT DE CORPS.** "Union is strength." Harmony, union among the personnel of a concern, is a great strength in that concern. Effort, then should be made to establish it.

Management By Exception Principle:

The **Management By Exception Principle** is widely applied to the controlling function of management. In essence, it says that a manager should spend his or her time only on those areas that demand personal attention. The routine should be delegated to others and procedures established to deal with it. When exceptions occur, they are usually situations for which there are no precedents and then the manager's attention is warranted. Where controls reveal exceptions for which there are no prescribed solutions, the manager must take action.

Objectivity Principle:

The **Objectivity Principle** is necessary for managerial effectiveness. Objectivity is the ability to be relatively unbiased and not limited to excessive personal prejudices or perspectives. Managers who possess this objectivity are able to see the other person's point of view. This is very useful when dealing with a conflict between two subordinates. Since it recognizes that everyone has biases and reacts in a way that makes sense to them, it is up to the manager to clarify positions and resolve the conflict in a way that meets the total organization's goals.

Adaptability Principle:

Adaptability is important to the manager who must work in a constantly changing environment. Developments in technology, an abundance of information, changes in personnel and legal restrictions, and demands of organizational climates confront managers today. In view of these conditions, managers must adopt and keep a positive attitude, a receptivity to new information, and maintain regular flexibility when responding to challenging problems and situations. Rarely can a manager rely entirely on a single management approach to all situations. It is mandatory that managers focus on the benefits of continuous change and learning for the benefit of the entire organization, themselves, and their employees.

Administrative-Conceptual, Human, and Technical Skills:

Overall, managers must develop and balance their application of their administrative-conceptual, human, and technical skills:

* **Administrative-Conceptual Skills.** Knowledge of the total organization and how it is structured and coordinated; knowledge of its information and records systems; an ability to see the whole picture, conceptualize, and think in the abstract when planning, organizing, and controlling work.

* **Human skills.** Knowledge of human behaviors, needs and motivations, and an ability to work effectively with diverse individuals and groups,

including peers, superiors, and subordinates; encompasses interacting with subordinates, communicating, leading, motivating, delegating, problem solving, and decision making.

* **Technical Skills.** Job know-how; knowledge of the industry and it's particular processes, procedures, equipment, systems, and problems.

Managers should pay as much attention to human relations matters as to technical and administrative concerns. Many times managers emphasize productivity, results, and task accomplishment in the short run and neglect employee-centered interests and relationships with employees for the long run. Studies by Rensis Likert and others have generally concluded that managers who focus on job demands to the EXCLUSION of their interest in the welfare and the development of their people do not get the results they desired. Conversely, managers who overly emphasize easy work and friendships do not get optimal results either. The key is a balance between the concern for work and the concern for people and the appropriate applications of the related skills. Generally, the supervisory role emphasizes human and technical skills most and administrative skills least.

Group Dynamics, Organizing, and Team Building

Effective Group Criteria, Conditions, and Behaviors

Initially, the genuine meaning of effectiveness or success must be determined for any organization, work group, team, individual, or even any piece of equipment or entity. What makes an individual manager, an employee, or an organization or work group "Effective?" What are the expectations, conditions, or criteria which must be met? Of course, the criteria must be defined and applied relative to a given, unique situation, its conditions, the present environment, and the total, long-run, big picture. It is important to note over the long run that all six elements must exist for total effectiveness, even though tradeoffs must be made among the elements in short run situations. As a working definition for *"Effectiveness"* and based on his research, the author wants to offer the following six general criteria or elements of long-run effectiveness for individuals, organizations, or anything:

Findley's Elements of Effectiveness: EXHIBIT # 2

1) *OUTPUT*-- The *results* or production of the total system or entity over the long run. Actual accomplishments, achievements, attainments, and factual results, not potentials, must be defined and realized. Effectiveness of an organization can be determined in part by such things as completing a major project on time, producing a high quality product or offering a high quality service, realizing a significant cost savings for the organization, providing a high level of service to customers, and realizing the respect of peers and supervisors. Individuals can be effective in terms of actual attainment of their long-run goals, e.g. earning a college degree, having a successful marriage, achieving a specified level of financial security, holding specific job responsibilities, and developing themselves to given spiritual and physical levels.

2) *PRODUCTIVITY*-- *Output per person per period of time.* It is not enough to accomplish actual results and realize production over the long run, but the output realized must be in terms of what is produced by each individual, organization, resource, or entity and identified and related to a defined time period.

3) *EFFICIENCY*-- *Minimum input to get the maximum output.* It is not complete effectiveness to get results for a particular individual, organization, or entity, for a certain period of time, without striving to be efficient. Many times efficiency is taken to be synonymous with effectiveness, while it is only a part of total effectiveness. Utilization of the minimum resources and assets to accomplish the highest level of output, or efficiency, is a critical part of total effectiveness. If individuals increase output at a faster rate than input or cut back input faster than output, efficiency results. This conservation of the application of resources and inputs while realizing the maximum level of results is advantageous to the total organization.

4) *SATISFACTION*-- *Gratification* of personal needs and wants. Recognition, respect, and attention to the needs and wants of all

individuals involved in a situation and striving for consensus agreement on many (not all) issues and actions to accomplish a win-win result should be a goal for supervisors, especially over the long term. Positive fulfillment and acceptance of one's self and others contributes to total effectiveness.

5) *ADAPTIVENESS*-- Being *flexible* in all situations. Attempting to first understand others before advancing your own cause, issue, or action is necessary. Respecting and allowing for differences in needs, values, views, opinions, behaviors, processes, and positions of individuals, groups, and organizations takes time and effort, but significantly contributes to effectiveness for the total system.

6) *DEVELOPMENT*-- Focusing on continuous *growth* and learning. Actively seeking to regularly acquire knowledge and awareness of the breadth and depth of concepts, principles, skills, abilities, and behaviors applicable to many specific circumstances on the job and for life in general. Recognizing current limitations and striving for the top priority and dominance of personal maturation and self actualization in all aspects of your existence.

Aside from recognizing and accepting the elements of one's environment or situation which one cannot change, there are other elements which one must recognize, accept, and definitely strive to influence. To be effective as a manager of an organization OR as the manager of one's own life means coming to terms confidently, assertively, and maturely with three basic factors:

1) **Authority**. The right to live and act in ways of one's own choosing. Each individual has the authority to decide what to do with his/her life, how to organize it, whom to include in it, and how to manage it. We are the manager of our own destiny and have the authority to manage it.
2) **Responsibility**. The conscious acceptance of accountability to one's self for the consequences of one's action and for the present quality of one's life. An individual can decide for them self that they do not want to follow a certain course of action or behavior any longer and accept accountability for CHANGING it to improve their quality of existence.

3) **Choice**. The basic process of moving through life, making choices among known or created alternatives for action. Choosing consciously what to do in dealing with ANY specific situation, in order to meet your own goals and objectives. One must recognize the consequences of selecting a certain alternative over another one, which includes alienating another or not meeting someone else's goals, objectives, or expectation. An analysis of the positive and negative outcomes must be made by each individual in terms of their own goals, objectives, and expectations in any given situation. Certainly, the job situation and organizational goals and objectives affect those of the individual. One should strive to blend organizational and individual goals and objectives for mutual benefit, career advancement, and even maintenance of a job. When there are conflicting organizational and individual goals, objectives, expectations or values (and the individual does not CHOOSE to attempt to change either for whatever reason), one alternative to be analyzed and perhaps chosen is to move on and seek another career, job or organization for employment.

The six elements of effectiveness and the above related overall personal management factors suggest *four areas of human skills* which will help us to be personally effective on the job and in life in general (See Findley's 1986 Job Application, Interviewing, and Resume' Preparation book, 2nd edition):

1) **Mood Control**. The psychomotor skill of maintaining a positive frame of mind, attitude, and a correspondingly positive emotional bias in the vast majority of situations one encounters.
2) **Self-actualization**. Planning, organizing, and implementing one's life in such a way as to get what one really wants, rather than what one thinks others will approve of; actualizing one's own values, philosophy, and skills to become everything that one is capable of becoming to the fullest extent possible in all areas of life (a gigantic challenge).
3) **Social Competence**. The various skills which enable one to get what one wants in dealing with other people AND to maintain positive and rewarding interactions with them over the long term, while respecting them and their individual differences.
4) **Practical Results and Actions**. The useful, pragmatic, everyday

behaviors and skills of getting win-win results and outcomes through creative problem solving, realistic decision making, making plans, setting objectives, monitoring one's progress, getting one's self and one's personal affairs well organized, and taking timely action to get things done, rather than procrastinating. *Self awareness significantly contributes to effective behaviors and accomplishing quality personal and organizational results and overall effectiveness in life.*

Restructuring:

In order to decrease costs, managers have been restructuring organizations to reduce the number of employees on the payroll. **Restructuring** involves downsizing an organization or reducing its operations by eliminating jobs of large numbers of managers at all levels, as well as non-managerial workers. Restructuring enhances efficiency by allowing the organization to make better use of its remaining resources and by reducing costs. However, restructuring can produce some powerful negative outcomes. It can reduce the morale of remaining workers, who may be worried about their own job security. Some top managers of downsized organizations are realizing that they have downsized too far, because customer complaints about poor quality products and services have increased. Some managers in downsized organizations have discovered that they have to assume responsibilities of those who have left and are under increased pressure to perform several functions and specific tasks previously done by others, while still performing their usual work and monitoring and coordinating workers.

Empowerment and Self-Managed Teams:

A major change at the first-level of management has recently taken place to reduce costs and improve quality. First-line managers who typically supervise the employees engaged in producing goods and services are **empowering** their workers by expanding their tasks and responsibilities. Certain decisions are pushed down in the organization to the level of worker who is directly involved with the task. Another change is the creation of **self-managed teams** or groups of employees who are given responsibility for supervising their own activities and for monitoring the quality of the goods and services they provide. Members of self-managed teams assume many of the responsibilities and duties previously performed by first-line managers. First-line managers act as coaches or mentors whose job is not to tell employees what to do, but to provide advice and guidance to help the team find new ways to perform their tasks more efficiently.

Diversity:

The increased participation rate of women, Hispanics, Asian, Pacific Island, and African people in the workforce has changed its makeup and characteristics. As organizations become more heterogeneous in terms of gender, age, race, religion, and ethnicity, management has been adapting its human resource practices to reflect those changes. Many organizations today have work force diversity programs which tend to focus on training employees to increase awareness, understanding, and respect for *individual differences* and modifying benefit programs to make them more family-friendly. Managers must recognize the need to treat all human resources in a fair and equitable manner and the performance-enhancing benefits of diverse skills and experiences available from different kinds of people.

Bases for Diversity

A workforce is diverse when it is composed of two or more groups, each of whose members are identifiable and distinguishable based on demographic or other characteristics. The following are *bases* upon which groups can be distinguished:

- **Racial and Ethnic Groups.** About 25% of the U. S. Population.

- **Women.** Almost two-thirds of the 15 million new entrants into the job market in the 1990s will be women, making them the largest and fastest-growing diversity group.

- **Older Workers.** By the year 2000, the average age of the U.S. workforce will be 39, up from the 1998 average of about 36 years of age, reflecting the gradual aging of the workforce and the larger number of older people remaining at work.

- **People With Disabilities.** The Americans With Disabilities Act makes it illegal to discriminate against people with disabilities who are otherwise qualified to do the job, and this act has focused on the large number of people with disabilities in the workforce.

- **Sexual-Affectional Orientation.** About 10 percent of the population is gay, which may make gays a larger percentage of the workforce than some racial and ethnic minorities.

Barriers in Dealing With Diversity

The following are diversity barriers which may prevent an organization from taking full advantage of the potential in its diverse workforce:

1). STEREOTYPING & PREJUDICES. Stereotyping is a process in which specific behavioral traits are ascribed to an individual based on his or her apparent membership in a particular group. Prejudice is a bias that results from prejudging someone on the basis of some trait. Most people form stereotyped lists of behavioral traits that they identify with certain groups. Unfortunately, many stereotypes carry negative connotations and are inaccurate. When someone allows stereotypical traits to bias them for or against someone, then we say the person is prejudiced.

2). ETHNOCENTRISM. This is prejudice on a grand scale, since it views members of one's own group as the center of the universe and views other social groups less favorably than one's own. One who holds this perspective behaves with considerable bias and discriminates against those in the other supposedly inferior social group. The individual may not even realize nor understand that his or her behavior is so prejudiced.

3). DISCRIMINATION. This refers to taking specific actions toward or against the person based on the person's group. Of course, many forms of discrimination are illegal in the United States, e.g. discrimination against someone solely on the basis of an individual's age, race, gender, disability, or country of national origin.

4). TOKENISM. This refers to the tendency of some organizations to appoint a relatively small group of women or minority-group members to high-profile positions, rather than more aggressively achieving full work-group representation for that group. It is a diversity management barrier because, in part, it slows the process of hiring and promoting more members of the minority group and may discount the expertise of others. Also, "token" workers often perform poorly in the organization because of their lack of expertise for the particular position appointed to, the recognition by other workers of their lack of certain skills, and the resulting obstacles to full participation, success, and acceptance in the organization.

5). GENDER ROLES. Women in the workforce confront gender-role stereotypes or the tendency to associate women with certain types of jobs, usually non-managerial ones and ones in an office environment. Education programs and strong top-management leadership can assist in changing an organization's culture, management practices and system to overcome gender stereotyping. *Mentoring* or establishing relationships between a younger and an older, more experienced adult where the mentor provides support, guidance, and counseling to enhance the protégée's success at work and in other life areas can contribute to overcoming gender stereotyping and help with diversity management.

Group Development and Organizational Politics

<u>Stages of Group Development:</u>

It is helpful for a manager to understand the stages of the development process for a group, so that objectives, tasks, and performance can be appropriately determined and monitored.

Two key variables are used to determine where in the four stages of group/team development a particular group/team is. These variables are productivity and morale. "Productivity" in this sense means how competent the group is in completing tasks, while "morale" relates to the group's commitment, confidence, and cohesion. The stages are:

Stage 1, Awareness/Forming/Orientation. During this stage, productivity is low and goals are unclear. Skills and knowledge as a team are undeveloped. Morale is relatively high since members are eager and have positive expectations for the group. Group members are dependent on the manager/leader and have some anxiety about their individual roles and relationship to the group. Members may be quite superficial, reserved, and hesitant to participate.

Stage 2, Conflict/Storming/Dissatisfaction. In this stage, productivity increases slowly as the group's skills and knowledge start to develop. Morale, however, drops to a low point as initial hopes and expectations for the group are not easily met. Feelings of competition, frustration, and confusion are evident. Members bargain for position in the group.

Stage 3, Cooperation/Norming/Resolution. During this stage, productivity continues to increase as group skills and knowledge further develop. Goals become clearer or are redefined. Morale begins to improve as the group develops methods of working together. Negative feelings are resolved. Positive feelings and cohesion increase, and confidence as a group begins to develop.

Stage 4, Productivity/Performing/Production. During this stage, the team develops the skills and knowledge necessary to work well together and to produce desired results. Members have positive feelings about each other and the accomplishments of the group. The members are no longer solely dependent on the manager for direction and support; instead, each member assumes leadership roles as necessary. The team is high performing.

Characteristics of a High-Performing Team:

A high-performing team can be described by the acronym **PERFORM:**

Purpose. A common sense of purpose is shared by team members. They are very clear about what the team's "charter" is and why it is important. They can communicate what results the team intends to accomplish and what its goals, objectives, mission, and vision are. Strategies for achieving them are clear and each member understands his/her role in accomplishing them.

Empowerment. Members are confident about the team's ability to overcome obstacles and to realize its mission and vision. A sense of mutual respect enables members to share responsibilities, help each other, and take initiative to meet challenges. Members have opportunities to learn and to grow personally and through the organization. There is a sense of personal and group power.

Relationships and Communication. The team is committed to open and two-way communication. Team members feel that they can state their opinions, ideas, and feelings without fear. Listening is considered as important as speaking. Differences of opinion and perspective are valued, and methods of managing conflict are understood. Through honest and caring feedback, members are aware of their strengths and weaknesses as members. There is an atmosphere of trust and acceptance. Group cohesion is high.

Flexibility. Group members are flexible and perform different task and maintenance functions as needed. The responsibility for team development and leadership is shared. The strengths of each member are identified and used. Individual efforts are coordinated when necessary. The team is fluid and open to opinions and feelings, hard work, and fun. Members recognize the inevitability and desirability of change and adapt to changing conditions.

Optimal Results/Methods of Productivity. High-performing teams produce significant results. There is commitment to high standards and top-quality results. The team has developed effective and collaborative decision making and problem solving methods that result in achieving optimum results and in encouraging participation and creativity. Members recognize and respect individual differences and synergy and have developed strong skills in consensus and win-win approaches, the group process, and task accomplishment.

Synergy:

Many of a manager's daily encounters are with groups of employees or with employees within work groups and their is great dependence on the effectiveness of group effort. Synergy actually results from the combined action of two or more group members which produces an effect that is different and greater than the individual summation of the two or more individuals. In actuality, one plus one equals more than two. This result stems from the spinoff affect of blending two unique entities which combine in a special way in a complex situation to yield a result with compounded benefits. Managers must know the strengths and weaknesses of their individual employees and combine them to maximize work group effectiveness. Four factors are primarily responsible for collectively influencing work group effectiveness: (1) size of work group, (2) work group norms, (3) status of work group members, and (4) cohesiveness of the work group.

Group Cohesiveness:

The manager has considerable influence over the cohesiveness of the work group factor. Cohesiveness is defined as the attraction group members feel for one another in terms of desire to remain a member of the group and resist leaving it. The greater the cohesiveness that exists within a group, the greater the probability the group will accomplish its objectives and work tasks. Jeff Harris studied group cohesiveness and lists eight indicators of high group cohesiveness:

1) Members have a broad, general **agreement on the goals** and objectives.
2) Significant **communication** and interaction occurs in the group.
3) Members have a satisfactory level of **homogeneity** in social status and social background.
4) Members are allowed to **participate fully** and directly in the determination of group standards.
5) **Group size** is sufficient for interaction, but is not too large to stymie personal attention.
6) Members have a **high regard** for their fellow group members.
7) Members feel a strong need for the mutual benefits and **protection** the group appears to offer.
8) Group is **experiencing success** in the achievement of its goals and in protection of its values.

Organizational Politics:

Definition and Concept

When people get together in groups, power will be exerted and converted into actions to affect decision making in the organization or to influence behaviors that are self-serving and non-sanctioned by the organizational hierarchy. This is organizational politics and it is a fact of life in organizations. Politics seem to be more apparent in organizations whose resources are declining, when the existing pattern of resources is changing, and when there is opportunity for promotions. Organization cultures characterized by low trust, role ambiguity, unclear evaluation systems, high pressures for performance, win-lose approach to reward allocations, democratic decision making, and self-serving senior managers are more likely to contain political activity. While politics is fostered mostly by top-level managers, who themselves engage in political behaviors and thus create acceptable climates for continued politics, supervisors can influence organizational politics by being objective, logical, rational, and fair in their decisions and actions, according to organization-wide goals and objectives.

Organizational politics are often a positive force. Managers striving to make needed changes often encounter resistance from individuals and groups who feel threatened and wish to preserve the status quo. Effective managers engage in politics to gain support for and implement needed changes for the benefit of the total organization. Indeed, managers cannot afford to ignore politics even if they want to. By ignoring politics, they will not go away and managers will be unable to gain support for their goals and projects.

Strategies for Increasing Power

Managers who use political strategies to increase their power are better able to influence others to work toward the achievement of group and organizational goals. The following are strategies to increase a manager's power:

Controlling Uncertainty. Uncertainty is a threat for individuals and organizations and can interfere with effective performance and attainment of goals and mission. For example, job security threatens workers and may cause top performers to quit and take a more secure job elsewhere. Managers who are able to control and reduce uncertainty for others and the organization are likely to see their power increase. Managers gain power when they are knowledgeable about the projects, activities, and initiatives of the organization and can reduce or eliminate uncertainty in decisions and actions.

Making Oneself Irreplaceable. Managers gain power when they have valuable knowledge and expertise that allow them to perform activities or tasks that no one else can readily handle. Of course, the more central these activities and tasks are to organizational goals and effectiveness, the more power managers gain from being irreplaceable. For example, a computer systems analyst can have detailed technical knowledge instrumental to a major new system and cannot be quickly replaced.

Being in a Central Position. Managers who are in central positions and are responsible for activities that are directly connected to organizational profits, top-priority goals, and competitive advantage knowledge are usually involved with important communication networks both internal and external to an organization. Other individuals are dependent on them for their knowledge, advice, and support, and the success of the entire organization may be partly affected by them.

Generating Resources. To the extent that a manager is able to generate input resources (financial capital, skilled workers, and raw materials), technical resources (computers and machinery), and knowledge resources (marketing or engineering expertise) for an organization, that manager's power is likely to increase. For example, in universities, research professors who are able to win large grants to fund their research from national foundations gain power and earn respect because of their contribution to the whole organization.

Building Alliances. When managers build alliances, they develop mutually-beneficial relationships with individuals both inside and outside the organization. The parties support one another interests and both benefit from the association, providing the manager power because of the readily-available support without question that can be counted on for his or her initiatives.

Teams, Teamwork, and Consensus

A team is a formal work group whose goal is to generate synergy and improved collective performance through coordinated individual efforts. Teams have different needs and people should be selected for a team based on their personalities and preferences and what role they can fulfill for the team. High-performing teams properly match people to specific roles. Margerison and McCann in their 1990 book, Team Management: Practical New Approaches present nine team roles for creating high-performance teams:

Team Roles:

1) CREATOR-INNOVATORS-- Imaginative and good at initiating ideas or concepts. Are very independent and prefer to work at their own pace in their own way and very often in their own time to get results.

2) EXPLORER-PROMOTERS-- Like to take new ideas and champion their cause. Are good at picking up ideas from Creator-Innovators and finding their resources to promote these ideas. May not have the patience and control skills to ensure the ideas are followed through in detail.

3) ASSESSOR-DEVELOPERS-- Have strong analytical skills. At their best when given several different options to evaluate and analyze before a decision is made.

4) THRUSTER-ORGANIZERS-- Like to set up operating procedures to turn ideas into reality and get things done. Set goals, establish plans, organize people, and establish systems to ensure deadlines are met.

5) CONCLUDER-PRODUCERS-- Are also concerned with results. Take pride in producing a regular output to a standard. Focus on insisting that deadlines are kept and ensuring that all commitments are followed through on.

6) CONTROLLER-INSPECTORS-- High concern for establishing and enforcing rules and regulations. Are good at examining details and making sure that inaccuracies are avoided, want to specifically check all facts and figures.

7) UPHOLDERS-MAINTAINERS-- Hold strong convictions about the way things should be done and promote stability. Defend and fight the team's battles with outsiders while strongly supporting internal team members.

8) REPORTERS-ADVISERS-- Are good listeners and do not press their point of view on others. Favor getting more information before making decisions. Discourage hasty actions.

9) LINKERS-- Overlap the other roles and can be performed by any of the others. They try to understand all views and are coordinators and integrators. Dislike extremism and try to build cooperation among all team members. Try to integrate people and activities despite differences.

While most individuals can perform any of these roles, some are best suited to one particular role. The supervisor must understand the individual strengths of each person and allocate team work assignments accordingly, for maximum cooperation and effectiveness.

The Consensus Concept

Consensus decision making is a concept that supports team collaboration and group involvement based on having a shared purpose and trust among team members. Consensus fosters collaboration, trust, and involvement by compelling people to figure out creative ways to get everyone's needs met, so a beneficial win-win decision results.

In majority rule situations, as many as 49% of the team members may not agree with the decision. Sometimes these members will silence their input and will to further the team's goals and sometimes they will sabotage the process. Consensus is a preventive for sabotage and demands participation. Team effectiveness and trust can be hampered if a team member believes they can be forced into a decision or action they do not want. The consensus decision making process enhances trust and effectiveness by facilitating discussions, encouraging pro and con comments, and generating support from team members.

Consensus Definition

If a team decides to use consensus as the decision making model, it is imperative that the team develop its own understanding of consensus. Since not all decisions require the consensus decision making process, teams must decide what types of decisions require consensus. The conventional decision making process is usually adversarial, often reflects a desire for power and control, is hierarchal in structure, is characterized by linear thinking, the ethic is competition, and has the goal of unilaterally winning. At times and in certain situations and environments, this is appropriate. The government and the military make effective use of this process. Such a structure can pose formidable barriers to sustainable development, where the challenge is to integrate complex functions, achieve interdisciplinary cooperation, and satisfy diverse interests. Generally, consensus means that all team members get the chance to be heard and that the resulting decision represents the common opinion or viewpoint which is held by all or most of the team members. There is *"general agreement"* about the issue, process, and course of action. A decision is made that does not necessarily have 100% agreement among all team members, but a decision is made that all members support and can live with. The decision will not be blocked by any member. The consensus process takes longer than a conventional or arbitrary decision, but it is more meaningful and assures follow-through for implementing decisions over the long run. Decisions by consensus generally last after implementation, which can save a lot of time and resources for the long run, and build relationships. While there is agreement on all major points, issues, and team courses of action, there is not necessarily agreement on each sub issue and point. However, the resulting decision represents the entire group and unanimous agreement is presented.

Creating A Climate for Consensus

One of the challenges inherent in using consensus is creating an appropriate environment which supports dissent and encourages all members to speak their truth. When a person takes the enormous risk of speaking their truth in the consensus process, and their truth runs counter to the group, they need to be affirmed and supported, otherwise they will not share their truth and risk disagreement. There is always the false consensus possibility where what members say publically is not what they say privately in regard to group consensus. Another sign of false consensus is when a course of action, decision, or agreement is not followed, routinely ignored, or outright rebelled against. For consensus to function, everyone on the team has to agree that the overall purpose, mission, and existence of the team is more important than their own personal agenda. There has to be a commitment to the team. For consensus blocking to be reasonable, the blocker should believe that the proposed course of action is not in the best interests of the team. When someone blocks because it is not in the best interests of the team, a solution can be found by asking "Why does this course not serve the best interests of the team?" It is best not to default to voting for decisions, since every team member must voice their ideas, "buy in", and understand the alternatives for the course of action. Voting so the team can "move on to the next issue" does not resolve differences. Straw balloting can be used, however, to check to see if consensus is close. For example, one might say "Please raise your hand if you cannot live with and support this decision." Many times, there is agreement and you can stop the discussion. However, if some people cannot support the decision, you can ask them what it would take to get to consensus. Identify items where there is agreement. The individual who cannot agree with the team should state why he or she cannot agree: what is the specific conflict. The individual who disagrees should be expected to articulate an alternative plan or another possible solution. Although everyone should have the opportunity to participate in the consensus process, it does not mean that everyone will and must participate. However, if they do not participate for whatever reason, then they must support and trust the team as if they had participated. Make sure consensus is reached before moving on.

Types of Team/Group Behaviors

Individuals have both personal goals and objectives AND organizational goals and objectives. When interacting with other team members in an organization, individuals may exhibit any one of three types of *behaviors:*

1) **Task Behavior.** Focus on the jobs and specific activities the group/team is suppose to accomplish for the organization.

2) **Relationship/Maintenance Behavior.** Focus on how the team/group members relate to each other and their functional interactions within the organization and/or team/group.

3) **Self-Oriented Behavior.** Focus on meeting the individual's personal needs, which do not necessarily detract from nor contribute to the organization's nor team's/group's functioning, development, or goal accomplishment.

Self-oriented behaviors can lead to an ineffective team, if the individual sees a personal need, goal, or objective being frustrated and not achieved in the organizational setting AND his or her actions are incongruent with the organizational goals and needs.

Self-Oriented Behaviors

Aggressiveness: Showing hostility against the group or some individual; criticizing or blaming others; deflating the ego or the status of others.

Blocking: Interfering with the progress of the group by doing such things as going off on a tangent, citing personal experiences unrelated to the issue being dealt with by the group, arguing to extreme for or against a point, etc.

Self-Confessing: Using the group as a sounding board to express personal feelings or points of view that do not add value to the group's activities.

Competing: Vying with others to produce the best idea, generate the most alternatives, talk the most, play the most roles, etc.

Seeking Sympathy: Trying to induce other group members to be sympathetic to one's problems; deploring one's own situation and constantly complaining; disparaging one's own ideas to gain support, etc.

Special Pleading: Introducing or supporting suggestions related to one's own "pet" concerns or philosophies.

Seeking Recognition: Attempting to call attention to one's self by loud or excessive talking, extreme ideas, or unusual behavior.

Withdrawl: Acting indifferent or passive; resorting to formality; daydreaming; doodling, etc.

Misdirection: Disrupting the group by joking and clowning around; constantly diverting attention in a humorous way.

Assertive Behavior

Assertive behavior is a type of interpersonal behavior in which an individual stands up for his/her legitimate rights in such a way that the rights and feelings of others are not violated. This differs from both *aggressive behavior* which violates the rights and feelings of others, and *non-assertive behavior* which enables one's own rights to be violated.

Assertive behavior is the honest, direct, and non-hostile expression of one's feelings, opinions, and beliefs, while respecting the feelings, opinions, and beliefs of others. The latter prompts others to feel respected, while the former and latter together prompts them to reciprocate, which in turn makes it more likely that:

❏ Open, honest, sensitive, and empathetic verbal communication will occur;

❏ An atmosphere of mutual respect will develop;

❏ Interpersonal relations on an equal basis will evolve; and

❏ A realistic, constructive approach to the handling of disagreements will emerge.

It is important to remember and accept <u>assertiveness</u> as a characteristic of behavior which expresses an idea in a specific situation and is not indicative of that individual's holistic views, all of their personal values, or their total personality or worth as a human being.

<u>TEAMS ARE ALMOST ALWAYS BETTER SERVED BY THE WIN-WIN-WIN APPROACH OF ASSERTIVE BEHAVIOR.</u>

Managing Change and Interpersonal Relations

Change: Organizational and Individual Perspectives

Most agree that if any organization is to be successful and achieve its objectives, it must *continually change and adapt* to significant developments and changes in its environment, such as changes in customer needs, technological breakthroughs, and new government regulations. More and more organizations and individuals today face a dynamic environment, including more cultural diversity in the work force, the immediate availability of much information, advanced computer capabilities, global expansion and considerations, and rapidly changing world politics and related scenarios. Managers must accept change as natural and anticipate and work with its significant and pervasive elements.

<u>Change Process:</u>

In essence, managers and supervisors must recognize the need to change quickly, overcome individual and organizational resistance to change, develop and implement effective changes, and monitor and manage changes for their effectiveness. How managers deal with the major factors to be considered when changing an organization determines how successful an organizational change will be. The major factors in the change process are: (1) the change agent, (2) determination of what should be changed, (3) the type of change to make, (4) individuals affected by the change, and (5) evaluation of the change. The change agent is anyone inside or outside of the organization who tries to effect change, e.g. an internal manager or external consultant. The four key factors that might change, and which must be appropriately blended for organizational effectiveness, are:

* *structure*
* *people*
* *technology, and*
* *financial resources.*

Certainly, the organizational policies and procedures, the characteristics of the human resources, the type of equipment and processes, and the level and availability of funds significantly influence change. The highest degree of change in any one of the four key factors defines the overall type of change.

Responses to Change:

The human resources or people change has the greatest potential for increasing organizational effectiveness because it focuses on changing individual's behaviors, values, attitudes and leadership skills which directly determine the effectiveness of the other factors. There can be individual responses and organizational responses to change and both offer resistance to organizational effectiveness. RESISTANCE CAN ALWAYS BE EXPECTED WHEN A SUBSTANTIAL CHANGE IS PROPOSED. Individuals generally resist change because something is different that affects their habitual response, is a threat to their feeling of security, has the possibility of lowering their income, or because they fear the unknown. Organizational resistance sources include the fear of the limited focus of the change (change one subsystem but not others), the threat to established power relationships, the threat to established resource allocations, and the threat to the expertise of specialized groups or individuals.

Change Strategies:

Before finalizing change strategies, managers should systematically think about change in their organization. One useful framework for this is Kurt Lewin's **Force-Field Analysis.** Basically, he says that organizations change because of driving and restraining forces, neither of which is inherently good or bad, but require attention and response. Driving forces are those that promote change, growth, and development, e.g. a new technology and employee demand for a higher quality of work life. Restraining forces are those that promote organizational stability, the status quo, and that resist change, e.g. external groups who fight against change and internal groups who have a vested interest in maintaining the status quo.

A Learning Organization:

"Organizational learning" is the process through which managers seek to improve employees' desire and ability to understand and manage the organization and its task environment, so that employees can make decisions that continuously raise organizational effectiveness, according to Peter Senge in his 1990 book <u>The Fifth Disciple: The Art and Practice of the Learning Organization.</u> Argyris and Schon in their 1978 book <u>Organizational Learning</u> define a "learning organization" as one that has developed the capacity to continuously adapt and change. They view a "learning organization" as an effective organization that has a remedy for the three fundamental problems inherent in traditional organizations: fragmentation (due to specialization), competition (overemphasis undermines collaboration), and reactiveness (misdirects attention to short-term problem-solving and away from creating something new). In general, a *"learning organization"* that stimulates far-reaching organizational improvement has the following characteristics:

1) A shared vision that everyone agrees on.
2) People discard their old way of thinking and the standard routines for solving problems or doing their jobs.
3) All organizational processes, activities, functions, and interactions with the environment are thought of as a system of interrelationships.
4) People openly communicate with each other across vertical and horizontal boundaries without fear of criticism or punishment.
5) People sublimate their personal self-interest and fragmented departmental interests to work together to achieve the organization's shared vision.
6) A double-loop system for learning that corrects errors in creative ways that involve the modification of the organization's objectives, policies, and standard routines; challenges deep-rooted assumptions and norms within an organization.

Strategies for change in an organization can be focused on the key factors of structure, people, technology, task, and finances. Structure strategies include changes in departmentation or grouping of functions, an increase in decentralization of authority and responsibility, and a change in span of supervision or levels of management. People strategies include specific training and development activities, team building sessions to increase trust and openness, and development of process skills to improve empathizing, listening, communication, tolerance of individual differences, and conflict resolution skills. Technology strategies include computer systems applications, just-in-time systems, and materials requirement planning. Task strategies include redefining the mission and vision, changing the functional strategy, and job enrichment strategies. Finance strategies include allocating funds based directly on goal priorities, profits generated, or key projects or equally for all organizational units.

Organizational Development:

Organizational Development (OD) is a planned, organization-wide effort, managed from the top, to increase organizational effectiveness through planned interventions (change) in the organization's processes. Workers themselves formulate the change that is required and implement it, often with the assistance of a trained consultant.

OD Objectives

The typical *objectives of an OD effort* are:

1). To increase the level of trust and support among organization members.

2). To create an environment in which the authority of an assigned role is increased by personal authority based on expertise and knowledge.

3). To increase the level of personal and team responsibility in planning and implementation.

4). To increase the openness of communication between organization members.

5). To more frequently find synergistic solutions to problems.

OD Characteristics

The distinguishing characteristics of OD are:

1). **Based on Action Research.** OD involves a systematic, scientific process where data is collected about a department or organization and is then fed back to the workers, so they can analyze it and develop hypotheses about the problem definition.

2). **Applies Behavioral Science Knowledge.** The goal is to improve total organizational effectiveness through understanding the culture, needs, motivations, and other behavioral information.

3). **A Personal Change Process.** It changes the attitudes, values, and beliefs of workers so that the employees can identify and implement the technical, procedural, structural, or other changes needed to improve the organization's functions.

4). **An Organizational Change Process.** It changes the organization's processes striving for improved problem solving, decision making, responsiveness, quality of work, and overall effectiveness.

Key Equal Employment Opportunity Legislation:

The following is a summary of some of the key Equal Employment Opportunity legislation and actions that have *changed* the way American organizations are managed:

1). **Title VII of 1964 Civil Rights Act**, as amended in 1972. Bars discrimination because of race, color, religion, sex, or national origin; instituted EEOC

2). **Executive Orders 11246 & 11375.** Prohibit employment discrimination by employers with Federal contracts of more than $10,000 (and subcontractors); established Office of Federal Contract Compliance; require Affirmative Action programs

3). **Equal Pay Act of 1963.** Requires equal pay for men and women for performing similar work

4). **Age Discrimination in Employment Act of 1967.** Prohibits discrimination against a person age 40 to 65 in any area of employment because of age; restricts mandatory retirement

5). **Occupational Safety and Health Act of 1970.** Establishes mandatory safety and health standards in organizations

6). **Vocational Rehabilitation Act of 1973.** Requires affirmative action to employ and promote qualified disabled persons and prohibits discrimination on the basis of physical or mental disabilities against disabled persons

7). **Vietnam Era Veterans' Readjustment Assistance Act of 1974.** Requires affirmative action in employment for veterans of the Vietnam War era

8). **Pregnancy Discrimination Act of 1978.** Prohibits discrimination in employment against pregnant women, or related conditions

9). **Mandatory Retirement Act of 1978.** Prohibits the forced retirement of most employees before the age of 70.

10). **Employee Polygraph Protection Act of 1988.** Limits an employer's ability to use lie detectors

11). **Americans With Disabilities Act of 1990.** Strengthens the need for most employers to make reasonable accommodations for disabled employees at work; prohibits discrimination

12). **Civil Rights Act of 1991.** Reverses Wards Cove, Patterson, and Morton decisions; places burden of proof on employer and permits compensatory and punitive damages for discrimination

13). **Wards Cove v. Atonio; Patterson v. McClean Credit Union.** These Supreme Court decisions made it more difficult to prove a case of unlawful discrimination against an employer

14). **Morton v. Wilks.** This case allowed consent decrees to be attacked and could have had a chilling effect on certain affirmative action programs

15). **Griggs v. Duke Power Co.; Albemarle v. Moody.** Supreme Court decisions that ruled job requirements must be related to job success; that discrimination need not be overt to be proved; that the burden of proof is on the employer to prove the qualification is valid

16). **Family and Medical Leave Act of 1993.** Permits employees in organizations with 50 or more workers to take up to 12 weeks of unpaid leave for family or medical reasons each year

The Coaching Role for Managers

Sometimes workers need more than just technical training and basic managerial directive and evaluative interactions. They need the manager to coach them by helping them to improve their job performance by providing guidance, instruction, advice, and encouragement through informal, personal relationships. Effective managers are coaches, rather than bosses, who help workers refine their approach to things and improve the nontechnical side of their performance.

The first step in becoming a managerial "coach" is to make time available for meeting with your workers as individuals. If a manager thinks that he or she cannot spare the time, he or she needs to rethink his priorities and manage his time for the organization's most important resource: people. In order to know workers in depth, a coach should meet with each of them informally, face-to-face, at least once a month to:

(1) get to know each person as an individual;
(2) periodically update his/her knowledge about each of the subordinates;
(3) identify work and personal, work-related problems that you may be able to help resolve;
(4) learn how each subordinate is doing on the job; and
(5) show your concern for each subordinate's growth and improvement.

One coaching role is serving as a mentor to systematically develop and promote a subordinate's overall abilities through intensive tutoring, guidance, and assistance.

Constructive Confrontation:

A coach should develop specific abilities to analyze ways to improve an employee's performance and capabilities through constructive confrontation, active listening, showing genuine interest in the person as an individual, and observing the worker's behavior on a day-to-day basis. It's the coaches responsibility to reduce barriers to development and facilitate a constructive climate that encourages performance improvement. The climate should allow a free and open exchange of ideas, focus on mistakes as learning opportunities, express the manager's value of the worker's contribution to the unit's goals, and be positive and encouraging.

Hidden Agendas:

The managerial coach must be open and honest with the worker and not have a hidden agenda or indirect purpose for the informal relationship. The manager must get to the root of the problem and not hesitate to bring it up for discussion. A collaborative style of joint involvement without hidden agendas will encourage individuals to identify and choose among alternatives and actions.

Focus on Issues, Not Blame:

In work and interpersonal conflicts, one party naturally attempts to blame the other for what has happened. Quite obviously, each party feels that the other is wrong. However, the real issue is not WHO is wrong, but WHAT to do about it. The manager must focus on the problem, the issues, and how to resolve them with the workers' involvement. The more active a part the subordinate can take in appraising the problem and issues for himself and in outlining possible courses of action, the more committed he will be to the solution and more growth will occur. The manager should help each party develop for themselves a plan of action, not tell them what to do nor solve the problem for them.

Focus on Mutual Benefits, Not Win-Lose:

The participants in the problem situation should be parties to its solution. Both parties should benefit in the problem resolution and implementation of the solution in a win-win manner. One individual should not sacrifice so the other can benefit, but rather a collaborative effort for consensus should result. Once a problem has been identified and solved, the manager should work to get both parties to agree on how to prevent it in the future for the primary benefit of the organization. Thus, a win-win-win situation should be sought by the manager for the benefit of the two individuals and the organization.

Time Delay Value:

Sometimes the problem is much more serious than just one or two work groups that cannot get along. If the matter is extremely critical, the manager may need to have two or three meetings with the groups and may also need to check with his manager in deciding what to do. Other information may surface from others involved. Additionally, even if one solution does seem to be the best, the manager is wise to give it some thought before quickly implementing it. Thus, delaying an initial solution to a critical problem for just a few hours to reflect on it and consider its effect on key individuals and units is usually best.

The Counseling Role for Managers

Problems with worker performance can often be attributed to troubling personal factors that arise from conditions not related to the job and which disrupt or distract from the normal operations of the organization. For managers, this is a difficult problem area which cannot be overlooked and is a challenging counseling role. Problems with job performance which do not meet established standards of output or quality are routinely dealt with as they occur and during performance appraisals. However, personal problems which affect job behaviors and performance are more difficult to identify and resolve by the manager.

The Performance Counseling Concept:

The manager must accept the responsibility for workers who become problem performers, if their behavior effects the accomplishment of organizational goals and objectives. The manager has a continuing responsibility to confront worker behavior that affects productivity. Workers under stress often function far below their capabilities, may disturb the productivity of others, and hinder the mission and results. Eventually, many of these troubled workers become the subject of disciplinary actions and grievances, so it is best for the manager to recognize these personal problems early and intervene. For many workers, the distinction between problems arising from their personal lives and those associated with their work becomes increasingly blurred and the manager, as a third party, can assist. The goal is to **help the worker solve his or her own problem** by positively focusing on specific job-related behaviors and conditions which affect results.

Specific Signs of A Troubled Worker:

Workers who are personally troubled and become problem performers usually have a difficult time adjusting to work life as well as home life. Most people encounter periods in their lives when adjustment is difficult and their job performance may suffer. This is usually a temporary condition, so the manager must deal with it and should be careful not to quickly stereotype and categorize the troubled worker as a permanent troublemaker or as seriously emotionally disturbed. When the troubled state becomes serious and persists, there is a good chance that the troubled individual is suffering from a problem with an emotional, rather than a physical cause. It is best to refer this type of individual to a professional for diagnosis and help.

The manager must regularly deal with troubled workers whose difficulty in adjusting is both temporary and chronic in nature, but NOT those with psychotic and seriously neurotic disorders. So the manager can know what to do to assist troubled workers, the following are specific **signs of a personally troubled worker:**

1) Sudden change of behavior or usual attitude or mood.

2) Increased absences from work and more sick leave visits to avoid reality.

3) Increased accidents due to inattentive behaviors.

4) Irritability and perpetually dissatisfied because of belief that world is against them.

5) Reduced productivity, work slowdown, and increased rework for no apparent reason.

6) Preoccupation and daydreaming appearance due to focus on personal problem.

7) Increased fatigue and tiredness due to excessive worry and/or physical problem.

Clarification of Performance Standards:

Since the manager's goal is to help the worker and to focus on specific, job-related problem conditions, initially managers must establish an empathetic atmosphere to reassure the worker that they want to help them keep their job and are not out to punish them or get rid of them. Since this is a counseling session to provide help and not a disciplinary session for punishment, the manager should try to put the worker at ease. Because emotionally-troubled workers with personal problems are already fearful and angry they do not need additional pressure from managers, so managers must genuinely project this conviction of helping them. With empathy established as a foundation, managers can proceed to give the troubled worker opportunities to help themselves. The next step is to state the work-related goals or performance standards and assertively state the expected standards of performance on the job.

The manager should relate specific job-related examples of performance problems and NOT introduce anything whatsoever about personal problems. By honestly letting the personally troubled worker know how much the current distress is affecting the job and how much can be tolerated, in a caring and concerned manner, you are helping the individual and the organization. If the worker voluntarily brings the personal problem to the manager, the manager can help most by actively listening and helping the individual think through possible solutions to the problem. Sometimes troubled workers just want someone to be available and listen to their problem as they think it through aloud. It is critical that the manager NOT evaluate but listen, without interrupting, giving solutions, advice, or preaching.

Counseling vs. Disciplinary Action:

Just as counseling deals with personal problems which affect job performance, discipline deals with work and organizational behaviors and problems which affect job performance. Properly administered discipline corrects as well as punishes and helps to develop self-control among workers. Discipline should always come after counseling sessions to help the individual, after the worker is made aware of the problem behavior's effects on job productivity, and after all else fails. The main purpose of performance counseling is to help the worker solve his or her own problem, while the main purpose of discipline is to encourage workers to meet established standards of job performance and to behave sensibly and safely at work. Managers should think of discipline as a form of training and, of course, self-discipline is the best discipline. Discipline should be done in private and should not be used as a show of authority or power by the manager.

Basic Counseling Function:

If counseling is successful by the manager, the worker, not the manager, solves the problem. It is important that the manager take the time to give undivided attention to the worker and allow the worker time to orally explore and express his or her problem. Thus the primary function of the manager in counseling is to *LISTEN* patiently to what the worker has to say before making any comment. Managers should never argue with a worker while counseling, look beyond the mere words said to discover deeper meanings, and allow the worker to control the direction of the counseling session. This is a necessary and time-consuming process, but well worth it for the most important resource of the organization, the human resource. It is important that managers remember that they are not psychologists, social workers, or psychiatrists and that they can possibly do more harm than good if they attempt professional diagnosis and rehabilitation, offer hasty advice, or corrective action beyond their training, education, and experience. The providing of emotional first aid is a primary managerial role in counseling.

Guidelines for Worker Counseling:

1). Create a non-threatening and supportive environment for discussion. Establish a climate in which the worker will be comfortable and that will encourage him or her to be open and honest.

2). Let the worker know up front that the organization is primarily concerned with job-manifested work performance. Focus on the work problem and NOT the personal issue.

3). Explain in very specific terms what the specific worker needs to do in order to perform up to expectations on the job. Do not permit name-calling or placing of blame on others.

4). Actively listen patiently to what the worker has to say before making any comments of your own. Do not discuss personal problems during the session unless they occur on the job or unless the worker brings them up. Do not be influenced or misled by emotional pleas, sympathy tactics, or hard-luck stories; refrain from criticizing and arguing with the worker.

5). Refer the individual for professional help if adjustment is beyond the supervisor's limits.

6). Help the worker develop his or her own plan of action for dealing with the problem. Do not solve the problem for the worker.

7). Ask key open-ended questions and restate the worker's views, but resist telling what to do or how to do it. Do not diagnose.

8). Allow the troubled worker to control the direction of the session.

9). Summarize what has been said and agreed upon; explain that the counseling session does not offer any special privileges or exclude the worker from later standard disciplinary actions.

10). Seek commitment from the worker to implement the worker's decisions and course of action. Pledge to help the worker to succeed.

Conflict Resolution

Conflicts occur in organizations whenever the goals, objectives, methods, or interactions of two or more parties are in opposition. A certain amount of conflict is inevitable in any organization because of the complexity of organizational missions, goals, and worker interests and priorities. While each type of conflict is likely to have unique causes, most can be traced to goal incompatibility, competition for scarce resources, task interdependencies, and the organizational line and staff structure. A limited amount of conflict can be helpful, serve functional purposes, and should not be eliminated. Conflict can keep the work team self-critical, creative, and viable. For example, disagreement about a work unit's objective may lead to discussion, research, and ultimately generate a new and better objective. Excessive conflict may be dysfunctional because it may lead to interpersonal strife and interdepartmental bickering. One of the biggest problems for a manager is recognizing the symptoms of conflict and learning to determine the type of conflict situation, either functional or dysfunctional.

Dealing With Opposition To Your Ideas:

As a manager you may have goals that conflict with those of others you work with. Your department goal of high quality personal service might conflict with another department's goal of increased output. Even within your department two workers can disagree on how to provide the high quality personal service and be in conflict. Your overall approach to opposition as a manager is to maintain a win-win philosophy and make the solutions to conflicts and problems beneficial to all parties. Certainly, this is a herculean task, but not insurmountable.

Interpersonal Conflict Resolution Styles:

The interpersonal conflict between workers is by far the most critical and difficult type of conflict for a manager to deal with. There is no single approach to managing conflict under all circumstances nor even in most situations. Managers need to use the strategy that best fits the specific conflict situation they are trying to manage. Thomas identified the two primary conflict-handling dimensions as **cooperativeness** (the degree one party attempts to satisfy the other party's concerns) and **assertiveness** * (the degree to which one party attempts to satisfy his or her own concerns). With these dimensions, *five conflict resolution styles* can be used:

* AVOIDANCE. The manager (or worker) ignores the conflict and does nothing. The individual hopes the conflict will just go away or resolve itself. An individual may want to withdraw from or suppress the conflict or avoid others with whom they disagree. Sometimes conflicts do go away, but this is a risky strategy because if it does not go away, it may

be much more difficult to deal with at a later time. This style may be appropriate when there is a need to gather more information, the conflict is trivial, and when the supervisor perceives there is little chance of affecting the outcome.

* **ACCOMMODATING.** This is a smoothing approach where one party seeks to appease the other by placing the opponent's interests above his or her own. The individual attempts to get along with the other at all costs. One party is self-sacrificing in order to maintain the relationship, despite reservations, because the issue is minor and does not warrant a confrontation that could harm the more valuable relationship. This style may be appropriate when the individual realizes he or she is wrong, the issue is more important to the other party, maintaining harmony is the top goal, or it is important to allow the other to experience winning.

* **COMPROMISING.** This style is the most common approach used in conflict resolution. It selects a solution that satisfies some, but not all, of the needs of both parties in a conflict. This middle-of-the-road style may not always be the optimal solution, since each party both wins and loses to some degree. Each party gives up something and neither will be completely satisfied. It may be convenient and on the surface appear to be win-win in nature, but it can reflect a manager's weakness or lack of commitment for implementing the best solution. It should be avoided for critical issues for your work unit. It can be used when opponents with equal power are strongly committed to mutually exclusive goals and when workable solutions to complex issues must be achieved, especially within time constraints.

* **COMPETING.** When one person seeks to satisfy his or her own interests, regardless of the impact on the other party, this power-oriented style is used. It results in a win-lose situation. Competitors strongly assert their viewpoint and show little tendency to cooperate with the other party. Their is intention to achieve one's goal at the sacrifice of the other's goal or to convince another your conclusion is correct and theirs is mistaken. This style may be appropriate when you are convinced that you are absolutely right on an important issue, when something must be done a certain way, or when an important but unpopular action must be taken.

* **COLLABORATING.** When the parties in conflict each desire to fully satisfy the goal or concern of the other party, with a high degree of cooperativeness and assertiveness, with a mutually-beneficial outcome, the collaborative style is optimal. The intent with this style is to solve the problem by mutually defining the issue and objective, discussing differences, and incorporating valid insights of both parties, rather than by accommodating various points of view or compromising key points. This win-win style is the most productive strategy in the long run. It takes time to develop a solution that benefits both parties, but morale will be enhanced and there will be commitments for making the solution work. There must be a willingness by the parties to work through the conflict in a constructive and supportive climate, which is difficult in the heat of an argument. Collaboration is useful when parties to the conflict are mutually dependent, support for an agreement is required, and the use of creative resources is important. It is NOT appropriate when the issue is not important enough to warrant the time and energy required for this style, when the parties distrust each other, nor when the parties lack the skills necessary to collaborate.

Situational Considerations:

When resolving conflicts, supervisors need to gather as much data and information as possible and consider all the relevant factors present in the particular situation they are dealing with. If the manager is aware of the worker's characteristics, skills, and needs, as well as his or her own skills, values, goals, and abilities, then the situational considerations must also be considered in resolving the conflict. The situational factors include such things as the way the organization is **structured** with its departments, levels, and reporting **relationships**; the **policies, procedures,** rules, and decision making practices which govern the way work is accomplished; the extent the **tasks** of the particular job are defined and directed by the supervisor; the nature of the specific **problem or issue** (whether the issue or relationship is the priority) in relation to the surrounding influences on it; organizational **channels of communication**; the relative **power** issues of those involved; and the situational **time** pressure.

Collaboration Skills:

When intervening in conflicts between individuals, managers must demonstrate collaboration skills. The objective is to achieve a *mutually-beneficial resolution* to the conflict.

Initially, it is important to quickly stop any name-calling or destructive bickering, suppress emotions, and get the individuals to calm down. Separating the individuals physically apart is a good first step. Next, when meeting with the individuals to determine the nature of the conflict, it is important to objectively **listen** and depersonalize the conflict so that energies are not devoted to defeating each other. The supervisor must get both parties to see the goals, beliefs, and feelings of the other as legitimate through a **rational problem solving approach**. Finding common areas of agreement is a starting point. **Empathy** is a collaboration skill for the manager and the involved parties. Participation by each party in calmly, not emotionally, summarizing and **communicating** their position is key. The supervisor should also participate by summarizing what was said, without making judgments. In any conflict, **involvement** by the parties in expressing their views without interruption and seeking understanding of the other is necessary. **Tolerance** and understanding of differences in others is mandatory. Having each party restate the other's position or jointly list factual advantages and disadvantages of each position is one approach. The manager must control the conflict situation and avoid "we-they" confrontations or stereotyped insinuations by focusing on the specific issue and **factual** data. "Either-or" decision alternatives should not be presented. Seek mutual understanding and **win-win** outcomes. The following *hints* are offered for resolving conflicts:

* Remain calm and objective; control your emotions
* Use a problem solving approach and focus on the problem and issue, not people and personalities
* Gather and report factual supporting data and information
* Avoid absolute choice situations and seek "consensus" agreement

* Listen more than talk
* Seek mutual understanding and win-win-win outcomes for all parties and the organization

EXHIBIT # 3

Techniques for Dealing With Specific Problem People:

The following interpersonal conflict resolution techniques adapted from Robert Bransom's book Coping With Difficult People are offered for your consideration in dealing with nine problem workers you may encounter. While these are general approaches to handling stereotypical interpersonal conflicts, each conflict situation and individual must be dealt with on a personal and case-by-case basis.

1) **The BULLY or TANK**-- This is the pushy person who is abrupt and intimidating. He will bombard you with his information and approach and roll over you and dominate you, since they want to accomplish things immediately.
TECHNIQUE: Stand your ground, both physically and mentally. Firmly and directly assert your position and ideas, but do not be aggressive. Focus on results and completion of tasks, since they also want to get things done. Be friendly, but firm. If they interrupt you, ask that you not be interrupted because you are prepared, results oriented, and you have not finished your presentation. Do not argue nor start a contest with them, they will probably win. Work WITH them to get outcomes.

2) **The SLY CRITIQUE or SNIPER**-- This individual criticizes you unfairly and makes backstabbing, cutting remarks. They also bully and intimidate you, but they operate covertly in a sly manner. They make you feel like a fool in front of others. Because you blocked them or challenged them in some way and they cannot do anything because they are not in control, they feel angry and try to cut you down and embarrass you.

TECHNIQUE: Bring the grievance or issue to the surface and objectively deal with it. Get specific about any legitimate problem by asking them direct questions and calling attention to their sarcasm. Perhaps, involve your group and get their input to see if they agree or disagree with the problem. Provide a rational and peaceful alternative to open conflict. Focus on the group's goal and purpose and get back on track. Call attention to the critique's attack and ask how it helps to accomplish the joint goal.

3) **The EXPLODER or GRENADE--** This out of control manipulator is superficial, very emotional, and unrealistic. He appears overeager and fears losing prestige. He gets very excited about a new idea or project, However, he may throw an adult temper tantrum and explode at any time if things do not go his way.
TECHNIQUE: Help them gain their self-control and self-confidence. Give them recognition and credit to satisfy their ego need. Get their attention by saying things like "I like your idea." Assist them in keeping their emotions in check by not making sarcastic fun of them, ignoring them, nor humiliating them in front of others. Watch your tone of voice and choose your words carefully, so as not to cause an emotional explosion. Show your genuine concern and take time out to allow them to calm down. Find out what triggered the explosion.

4) **The GRIPPER or CHRONIC COMPLAINER--** Nothing is ever right or acceptable to this individual. He complains and whines most of the time about everything and wants you to take action or do something to fix or solve their concern.
TECHNIQUE: You want them to get involved and solve their own problem. Switch them to a problem solving process and get them to be analytical. Help them to define the problem, state their objective, think rationally, orderly, and systematically. Do not agree with their complaints, but listen to them, even if you are impatient. You probably will have to interrupt their string of complaints, but do so to acknowledge their main points. Summarize their gripes and then ask specific questions. Do not ask "why" questions, but ask direct and yes/no response questions to establish facts, e.g. "Have you told the individual how you feel?" Offer to set up a meeting for the two parties to allow them to resolve their problem. Use hard data and factual information to support your ideas, alternatives, and analysis.

5) **The PASSIVE CLAM--** This individual is non responsive and is the silent type. They never let you know where they stand on issues or projects and want to avoid controversy and friction at all costs. They withdraw, clam up, and say nothing. They are friendly, but you never know their ideas or positions.
TECHNIQUE: You must get them to open up by making it uncomfortable for them to remain silent and closed. Create an atmosphere where they can talk, usually a private or informal location. Have an expectant attitude that they will express their opinions or ideas and let them know you want to listen to them. Your silence with an expectant look is one possible approach. Humor is another possibility. Ask open-ended questions to permit them to elaborate and explain their position or ideas, e.g. "Tell me about that."

6) **The AGREEABLE CONFORMIST--** They speak up and will agree to any commitment, yet rarely deliver. They do not want a confrontation because they are afraid of disapproval by others. They want merely to conform to and be a part of the group. They seem to be very supportive, but do not produce the anticipated results. When they say "yes", it really means "maybe."
TECHNIQUE: You must make it safe for them to be honest by letting them know that their relationship is important to you and that they can trust you. Also let then know that you are counting on them and that you do not want to be let down in your relationship with them. Surface the problem and ask questions. Ensure you get a commitment from them.

7) **The NEGATIVIST--** The "no way" person. They are pessimistic and inflexible and object to everything. They assume things will never work out and that the situation is impossible and hopeless.
TECHNIQUE: Do not argue with the negativist because they really believe and are convinced that things will not work out. You must use an analytical approach and take the time to specify the issue and alternatives. Clearly and specifically define the problem and help them analyze alternative courses of action based on defined criteria.

8) **The EXPERT BULLDOZER--** This individual knows it all and is an expert on everything. He has solutions ready for all of your problems and

charges ahead with them to solve your problems for you. Usually, they do know a lot and have much information, but do not listen well. They feel they need certainty to be secure from failure and punishment and have strong self-esteem and self-actualization needs.
TECHNIQUE: Listen to them and acknowledge their comments and suggestions. Summarize their ideas as expert opinions and show respect for them. Do not challenge their knowledge or authority head-on. Present your ideas and information as a detour to theirs. Use extensional questions to get them to consider your thoughts, e.g. "What do you think of ...?" or "Perhaps, consider this ...." Ensure your ideas are factually-based and supported.

9) **The PRETENDER or THINK-THEY-KNOW-IT-ALL--** They do not know it all, but pretend that they have the information and expertise. They care about prestige and truly believe what they are saying, but do not have the background, skills, or knowledge required. They give convincing presentations on the surface, but lack the necessary depth of substance. They are motivated by the esteem need for respect and recognition.
TECHNIQUE: Give them an out by letting them protect their dignity and self-worth by "saving face." Change the subject or state the facts and take a systematic, logical approach. Do not directly challenge them because they may resort to stronger defenses with unsubstantiated data and information. Charge them to assist by researching a subject and providing documented references.

Consensus and Win-Win:

As previously presented, the consensus and win-win concepts are compatible. Consensus decision making supports team collaboration by facilitating involvement and common agreement and support for the decision, which represents the entire group. In win-win situations there are high degrees of cooperativeness and assertiveness which result in mutually-beneficial outcomes and long-term effectiveness.

THE PROCESS OF EFFECTIVE COMMUNICATION

The Communication Process

Purpose

Communication is the process of transferring *meaning and understanding* in the form of ideas and information from one person to another. Thus, the communication is not effective if the intended information is not understood and does not have the desired meaning. About 70 percent of an individual's awake hours is spent communicating in the form of writing, speaking, reading, and listening. A manager probably spends closer to 80 percent of his or her time communicating, mostly performing oral communications. No group or organizational team can exist without communication. This author has experienced in his consulting work that the far majority of organizational and group performance problems are based on a lack of effective communication. An idea, value, goal, or any information or behavior, no matter how outstanding, is useless unless it is transmitted and understood by others. Although the process is elementary, it has many places for failure and we must constantly work at effective communication. The first step in learning how to communicate more effectively is to understand the elements of the communication process and where possible problems might arise. Subsequently, the role of feedback, nonverbal communication, and the barriers to effective communication must be understood.

Elements

There are four basic *elements* in the communication process:

1. **SOURCE/ENCODING--** The source is the sender and originator of the idea to be expressed who must be sure of what is to be communicated and controls the type, form, and frequently the channel of the message. Encoding is the process of putting information in some form that can be received and understood by another. It can be verbal, written, painted, nonverbal, or symbolic. The source must encode a thought based on his or

her skills, attitudes, knowledge, education, training, values, experiences, and characteristics. The source must think not only of what is going to be said, but also of how it will be presented to have the desired effect on the receiver.

2. **TRANSMITTING THE MESSAGE--** The encoded information constitutes a message which is transmitted over a channel. The channel is the medium through which the message travels. Some are formal established by the organization and others are informal and social. No matter what means you use, unless the message is sent, no communication will occur. Of course, just because a message is transmitted does not mean it will be received and understood.

3. **RECEIVER/DECODING--** The receiver is the object to whom the message is directed. This individual receives the symbols and translates and interprets them into a form that he or she can understand, decoding. Just as the encoder was limited by his or her skills, attitudes, knowledge, etc., the receiver is equally restricted.

4. **FEEDBACK--** The final link in the process is feedback. After the message has been received and translated, the receiver becomes a sender and may transmit a return message as a reaction and response to the originator, thus closing the communication loop.

Feedback

The sender can discover how well he or she communicated through feedback from the receiver. Without vital feedback, you do not know how your message was interpreted, understood, and how well you communicated with the receiver. Communication is an exchange and, if it is to be successful, information must flow back and forth from the originator to the receiver (feedback), or at least the sender must have some knowledge of the receiver's reaction. Feedback can be either verbal or nonverbal and may take many forms, including silence.

Common Barriers

When managers try to send messages, there are several barriers to effective communication that can enter into the communication process. Barriers can occur and exist in any of the elements of communication presented. When the source and receiver have different backgrounds and meaning for words, communication is difficult. But barriers to communication exist even when the source and receiver share common meanings and backgrounds. The following are common barriers to effective communication:

*   **Filtering**. Occurs when the sender manipulates information so it will be seen more favorably by the receiver, e.g. worker tells manager what she feels her boss wants to hear.
Another example of filtering is when the receiver weighs and interprets a message in terms of the characteristics of the individual who sends the message, especially his or her credibility and organizational status. We generally are more likely to accept a given message when we have a favorable attitude toward a sender and if it comes from an authority figure.

*   **Selective Perception**. Receivers selectively see and hear based on their needs, motivations, expectations, experience, background, and personal characteristics. They do not perceive reality, but interpret what they see and call it reality. Different individuals can perceive the same message in very different ways. The two primary factors that influence the way in which a stimulus is perceived are the level of the receiver's education and their amount of experience. The tendency to structure the world into a predictable pattern is called stereotyping, which limits our perceptions so we can not grasp the whole of a stimulus and, thus, automatically do not perceive and consider parts of an event.

*   **Emotions**. How the receiver subjectively feels at the time of receipt of the message will influence how he or she interprets it. Extreme emotions, such as depression or jubilation, are likely to hinder effective communication. In these cases, we likely will disregard our rational and objective thinking and substitute emotional judgments and affective responses.

* **Not Listening**. Our minds wander because we listen at an average of about 600 words per minute, which is four times faster than the rate we speak. To actively listen we must concentrate on what is being said without interrupting the other person. While we hear something, we do not necessarily pay attention, understand and make sense of what we heard. We typically retain less than 50 percent of an orally communicated message immediately after we receive it and only about 25 percent at the end of two months.

* **Evaluating**. Carl Rogers in his book On Becoming A Person observes that "the major barrier to mutual interpersonal communication is our very natural tendency to judge, evaluate, to approve or disapprove the statement of the other person or the other group." We regularly and quickly make value judgments about what someone says to us, hampering our concentration on the message content and the communication process. We can not focus on, absorb, and truly understand what the other person intends when we immediately evaluate what was said and begin our evaluative thinking and formulate our response.

* **Language**. Words mean different things to different people, since meaning is not in the actual words but in the individual. In an organization, workers come from diverse backgrounds, ages, education, and cultures and have different patterns of speech and language usage, even though all speak the English language. Senders incorrectly assume the words and terms they use mean the same to the receivers as they do to them, creating communication difficulties.

* **Information Overload**. Because our complex organizations are constantly and rapidly changing, given the new technologies and Internet access, workers have a greater need for and better access to information. This tends to overload our communication networks, increase the flow of non-applicable information and data, and distort communication. Supervisors should ensure that workers are not overloaded with too much information and data, by transmitting and making available only that which is critical and related to the performance of their jobs.

Organizational boundaries become less relevant as a result of electronic communication by cellular phones, pagers, facsimile machines, video conferencing, and E-mail, contributing to a greater volume and frequency of communications and problems.

Oral and Written Communication

Formal and Informal Channels

Formal organizational communication follows the line and staff lines of the organization and can be downward, upward, and lateral. Informal communication, the grapevine, does not follow organizational lines and follows the pattern of personal relationships among the organization members. Managers must be concerned with all channels of communication, but especially downward communication to workers and lateral communication to other departments to coordinate activities, as well as the grapevine.

The Grapevine

The grapevine or "rumor mill" is the informal network of communication or the unofficial flow of information about people and events. Information not official or required by organization policies, procedures, rules or job conditions is considered grapevine information. It is free to move in any direction, skip authority levels, and is likely to primarily satisfy team members' social needs and sometimes to facilitate tasks. The grapevine is not controlled by management, is used mostly to serve the self-interests of those people within it, and is perceived by workers as being more believable and reliable than formal communications from top management. It moves rapidly, selectively, and usually effectively.

The *grapevine* exists when:

* Important information is not communicated through formal channels;

* There is a need to make sense of limited or fragmented

information;

* Anxiety and insecurity exists about the future of jobs, organizational change, and job conditions; and

* Information the workers want to know is withheld from them.

We tend to think of the grapevine as being inaccurate, but it is estimated that over 75 percent of grapevine information is correct, according to Keith Davis in <u>Human Behavior At Work</u>. Workers naturally communicate with each other on the job, both within and outside of their work area, and during work hours and non-work hours at lunch and when on breaks. So it is natural and inevitable that the grapevine will exist. Managers cannot eliminate it, so they must learn to work with it. For a supervisor to deal with the grapevine, he or she must establish an open, two-way communication climate and be approachable. If workers are informed there will be less of a need to rely on the grapevine. If workers feel they can come to the supervisor because he or she listens, gives honest feedback, and shows empathy, they will rely on him or her for work-related information and discuss issues. Also, if the manager is approachable, workers will more likely bring new information to him or her, so the supervisor will be better informed about what is going on in the work unit and identify informal leaders. Of course, the grapevine can be detrimental to an organization because it can distort information, promote gossip, and spur false speculation and guessing about organizational activities. To minimize negative consequences of false grapevine information, distribute maximum information through formal organizational channels, provide it quickly, announce timetables for making important decisions, explain decisions and behaviors which may appear secretive, and openly discuss the good and bad possibilities of future organizational issues and activities. Certainly, the grapevine is an important and inevitable part of any organization's communication system and must be understood and utilized by the manager for organizational effectiveness.

Selective Perception

Understanding selective perception is an important part of effective communication, since it is a major barrier as previously presented. It occurs when workers block out new information, especially if it conflicts with what they believe. Thus, when they receive information they hear only those words that reaffirm their beliefs and ideas. They hear what they want to hear, so they will not be disappointed. Information that conflicts with preconceived notions either is not noted or is distorted to confirm the preconception. Managers should recognize and allow for three distinct elements of *selective perception:*

1) Workers will interpret and place meaning to a message in terms of their own unique experience, background, and how they have learned to respond;

2) Workers will interpret and place meaning to a message in such a way as to resist any change in their major personality attributes; and

3) Workers will tend to group and organize characteristics of their experiences, so that they can make whole patterns, draw conclusions, and see reality in their own terms.

To minimize the negative effects of selective perception, managers should try to send messages with **precise meanings.** Ambiguous words and symbols generally tend to magnify the detrimental outcome of the perceptual process on interpersonal communication. In addition, managers should take special efforts to **clarify and emphasize important points** in their messages, so they will not be misinterpreted and not understood. **Asking for feedback** will give the manager information from a worker with a different background and experience base than theirs to help create a larger viewpoint, stimulate dialogue, and foster two-way communication.

Status Differences

Every organizational worker, including managers, has a particular status which is determined by such factors as position, title, pay, rank, office size, credibility and reputation, education level, trust, and other factors. It is a natural tendency to size up, evaluate, and weigh a message in terms of the characteristics of the individual who sends it. Communication may be hindered when status differences exist between communicators. A supervisor, and all managers, have a major challenge and responsibility to overcome these status differences to ensure communication is effective for the benefit of the work unit and the entire organization.

Research by Roberts and O'Reilly has shown that we are more likely to accept a given message when we have a favorable attitude toward a sender. When managers are perceived as having a high credibility rating and can be trusted, workers are more likely to accept their messages, sometimes even blindly. So, supervisors from the very start of the relationship should initially attempt to create a genuinely credible and trustworthy climate with workers in their work unit, so they can be respected and trusted. By modeling effective behaviors and actions, managers can create a foundation for their acceptance, so they can effectively motivate, persuade, and direct the work efforts of workers.

Logical Reasoning Fallacies That Hinder Communication

Mistakes are made in communication when managers and workers attempt to draw conclusions and develop logical reasons to explain ideas, based on their incomplete or inconclusive information and data, with few or little facts, with emotional appeals, and with incorrect assumptions. The following are *reasoning fallacies* that hinder effective communication:

1). **Asserted Conclusions.** Conclusions are drawn from insufficient data and information. Too much reliance is placed on "samples of one occurrence" and from one's limited experience.

2). **Post Hoc Fallacy.** Is based on the assumption that because one event follows another in sequence, it is necessarily directly related and "caused" by the other event.

3). **Faulty Analogy.** Is based on the assumption that what is true of a simple or familiar situation is also true of a complex situation. For example, selling a house is as easy as selling a shirt.

4) **Non Sequitur Fallacy.** This has been called the old "apples and oranges" argument. Asserting that Bill will make a great hospital administrator because he was a good medical doctor, does not follow based on objective criteria.. Another common non sequitur in the earlier military services assumed that athletic prowess translated into leadership ability. Non sequiturs are conclusions that do not necessarily follow from the facts.

5). **Hasty Generalizations.** Results when a few examples or limited data are used as proof or support for an idea, but they are inconclusive and do not (or may not) represent the complete idea, argument, or situation.

6). **Faulty Dilemma.** Is the implication that no middle position or other alternatives exist, only the particular extreme position presented. For example, "we should either fight to win or not get involved at all." Like it or not, there are a considerable range of options to consider between two extreme positions.

7). **Stacked Evidence.** Is the tendency to withhold facts or manipulate support, so that the evidence points in only one direction. Quoting out of context is an example. The proof of the idea or position is intentionally limited with carefully selected facts and structured to present only the desired position.

8). **Loaded Question.** Is the practice of slipping in an assertion and passing it off as a fact during questioning. Asking "When are we going to stop sinking money into this expensive program?" asserts a lack of effectiveness in the program, but does not prove it. Consequently, the implied conclusion is illogical.

9). **Poor Compromise.** Many problems are satisfactorily solved through comparison, but one should avoid the tendency to accept the compromise solution as the optimal one in all, or even many, situations. Sometimes, it is the worst course of action. A compromise involves each party relinquishing something merely for the sake of a middle-ground resolution or expediency.

10). **Non-expert Opinion.** The use of an assumed authority to sway or attempt to sway someone's ideas or argument based on supposed position authority or an unqualified authority.

11). **Primacy of Print Fallacy.** Acceptance of the printed word as completely valid and reliable support just because it is written down and because it was expressed by an author in a print medium. Verbal nonsense can be easily articulated in written form and rise to the level of objective analysis because it is contained in the print media. Be skeptical and thoroughly critical of the printed word, as you would be of the spoken word.

12). **Emotional Appeal.** Obvious examples of this fallacy range from the use of emotionally-charged words to name calling. Less obvious examples include: a) using *reputation or precedent* as sole support; b) *glittering generality* or using a conclusion wrapped in an attractive label; c) using *catch phrases* to emotionally attract attention for support; and d) using the *bandwagon appeal* to get some to accept an idea or argument because "everyone else" is in support (on the band wagon) for it.

Strategies for Successful Communication

Understand Nonverbal Messages

Nonverbal communication (NVC) is sending and receiving information by some medium other than verbal or written, without using words to encode thoughts. It refers to behavior and bodily expressions that act as messages or impart additional information about verbal messages. Factors used to encode thoughts and provide meaning in NVC include gestures, vocal tones, pitch, volume, and inflections, facial expressions, eye contact, physical contact and touching, physical distance, posture, clothes, and body movements such as nodding the head, wrinkling the forehead, smiling, frowning, winking, shrugging shoulders, uplifted palms, hand salute, and staring. Michael Korda in his book **Power! How To Get It, How To Use It** says that nonverbal meanings have much to do with the power you are perceived to have. He even suggests that the nonverbal symbol of wearing a navy pinstripe suit communicates competency and authority, while being the first to leave a meeting for the restroom will cause others to perceive you as weak. NVC is very important since it frequently carries more weight and is more believable than verbal communication. However, because of the great amount of subjectivity involved, it is difficult to assess and deal with.

Generally, if there is a disagreement or conflict between the verbal and nonverbal communication, the NVC will be believed and accepted for meaning. Mehrabian's research concludes in his book <u>Silent Messages</u> that only 7 percent of a message's impact comes from its verbal content, with the rest being nonverbal impact, with 55 percent from facial content and 38 percent from vocal inflection and content. Nonverbal messages cannot be as readily disguised or controlled as verbal ones. For a manager this means that his or her nonverbal behavior may communicate a much stronger message to workers than information presented in his or her memo, policy statement, conversation, verbal instruction, or staff meeting statement.

The academic study of body motions has been labeled **kinesics** and refers to gestures, facial configurations, and other movements of the body.

Although it is a relatively new field with limited documented data and research support, it concludes that every body movement has a meaning and no movement is accidental. So through body language, they conclude that we can communicate that we are lonely, depressed, puzzled, indifferent, impatient, or available, for example. While we may disagree with this approach, it produces additional information to consider, but with guarded conclusions and applications.

Kiechel refers to **proxemics** and how people use the interpersonal space around them to convey messages. For example, standing close indicates intimacy while sitting at the head of the table is a sign of status and power. When a work group meets several times, workers will likely implicitly assign themselves to certain places to sit around the meeting table. The leader almost always sits at the head of the table and the second ranking person at the other end, with the others seated around the sides. If individuals are assigned to positions around the table on a random basis, the persons sitting at the ends will tend to act more forcefully than they usually do, according to Kiechel. Again, this is additional information for managers to consider, but with careful conclusions.

Develop Listening Skills

As was noted earlier, listening is a key initial requirement for effective communication, but most individuals listen at only a 25 percent level of efficiency. Understanding depends on listening and listening requires paying attention, interpreting, and remembering information. Several factors hinder effective listening. Perhaps the primary obstacle is an individual's free time while listening. Since the average person speaks at the rate of 125 words per minute and the average listener comprehends and thinks at about 400 words per minute, a lot of time is available for idle mind wandering. Most of us have acquired bad listening habits to fill in the idle time and do not use the excess thought time to review what has been said and think of questions. The following behaviors are associated with *effective listening skills:*

1) **Make eye contact.** The eyes are a major nonverbal communicator

and can be used to put the speaker at ease so he will feel free to talk and help the listener connect better with the speaker.

2) **Show interest in what is said.** Look and act interested and pay attention. Give the speaker your undivided attention, not fake attention, and actively concentrate on what is said. Affirmative head nods and appropriate facial expressions convey interest and attention.

3) **Confirm your understanding.** Explain your understanding of what was said by restating it in your own words and feeding it back to the speaker when the sender is finished, e.g. What I hear you saying is that...." These reflective statements confirm if you were listening effectively and verify the accuracy of your understanding.

4) **Avoid distractions.** Avoid actions that suggest your mind is somewhere else. Do not look at your watch, shuffle papers, talk on the phone, or play with your pencil, since this indicates you are not fully attentive and may be missing part of the message.

5) **Ask questions.** The active listener analyzes what was said and asks questions. This provides clarification, ensures understanding, and assures the speaker you are listening. Use excess thought time to review and think of questions, but be careful to not miss information sent by the speaker.

6) **Do not interrupt.** Let the speaker complete his main thought before you try to respond. Do not second guess where the speaker's thoughts are going. Do not form a rebuttal while the speaker is talking when you disagree with his thought, just let the information flow in.

7) **Listen for main ideas and concepts.** Before concentrating on facts and figures and before formulating a rebuttal, listen to discover the speaker's main ideas. Try to empathize with the speaker so you can better understand his points. Keep an open mind.

8) **Listen for key words and relevant detail.** After primarily listening for main ideas, listen for a few key words and relevant supporting details to help you understand the main idea.

9) **Mentally organize the material.** Try to find an organizational pattern in the speaker's message and use it to remember what was said, e.g. "my first three points are..." or "the pros and cons are...." You can later recall the information by remembering the pattern used.

10) **Hold your immediate evaluations.** Our natural tendency is to immediately evaluate everything we hear right away. Just let the ideas and information flow in at first and absorb it for understanding, rather than placing a value judgment on it. You can evaluate later.

11) **Do not overtalk.** You cannot effectively listen if you are talking when someone else is talking. We would rather speak our own ideas than listen to what someone else says, but we must interact and listen to others to acquire information for understanding and for organizational success.

Utilize Feedback and Follow Up

Feedback is information that facilitates the understanding and control of communications, enabling the sender to adapt or adjust messages for greater clarity and meaning. Feedback makes communication a two-way process, since the receiver becomes the sender and the sender becomes the receiver. Developing and supporting feedback involves more than following up on communications.

Richard Hodgetts in his book Effective Supervision presents the following six useful tips for improving effectiveness through *feedback*:

1) **Immediate Feedback is Important.** Immediate feedback serves to reinforce desirable behaviors and ensure it will be repeated.

2) **Supervisory Feedback Should Complement Work-Related Feedback.** Although workers know themselves how they are performing on the job, the supervisor should still take time regularly to let workers know that the person in charge knows and appreciates the work.

3) **Give Positive and Negative Feedback.** Praising workers is positive and necessary, but negative feedback is expected and desired by the

worker so performance can be improved. Supervisors should not hesitate to regularly give negative feedback for performance improvement, since it is better than the tendency to give no feedback at all.

4) **Give Verbal and Nonverbal Feedback.** A smile and pat on the back are OK, but specific verbal feedback must also be regularly given.

5) **Workers Remember First and Last Feedback.** Initial comments set the climate for what is to follow. Supervisors should begin positively with feedback, so the worker listens. Also, the last comments will be fresh in the worker's mind and should be a summary of expectations.

6) **Establish Two-Way Feedback.** Feedback should come from workers as well to generate work-improvement ideas. Supervisors should talk to workers daily and encourage discussion.

Guidelines for Effective Communication

The American Management Association has a time-proven *"Ten Commandments of Good Communication"* provided in their 1955 Management Review article:

1. **Seek to clarify your ideas before communicating.** The more systematically a manager analyzes the problem or idea to be communicated, the clearer it becomes. Good planning must consider the goals and attitudes of the audience.

2. **Examine the true purpose of each communication.** Ask yourself what you really want to accomplish with your message... obtain information, initiate action, change another's attitude? Identify your most important goal and then adapt your language, tone, and total approach to meet the specific objective.

3. **Consider the total physical and human setting whenever you communicate.** Meaning and intent are conveyed by more than words alone. Managers must be sensitive to the many factors which impact the communication and adapt to the existing environment.

4. **Consult with others, when appropriate, in planning communications.** Frequently, it is desirable or necessary to seek the participation of others in planning a communication or in developing the facts on which to base the communication. This lends insight and objectivity to your message and gets the needed support.

5. **Be mindful while you communicate of the overtones rather than merely the basic content of your message.** Your expression, tone of voice, your apparent receptiveness to the responses of others, etc. all have a significant effect on those you wish to reach. Your awareness of the fine shades of meaning and emotion predetermines in large part the reactions of your listeners.

6. **Take the opportunity, when it arises, to convey something of help or value to the receiver.** Consideration of the other's interests and needs from their point of view frequently points up opportunities to convey something of immediate benefit or long-range value to them.

7. **Follow up your communication.** Your best efforts at communication may be wasted, and you may never know whether you have succeeded in expressing your true meaning, if you do not see how well your message came across. You can do this by asking questions, by encouraging the receiver to express his or her reactions.

8. **Communicate for tomorrow as well as today.** Even though communications may be aimed at meeting immediate situational demands, they must be planned with the past in mind if they are to be viewed as consistent by the receiver. Also, they must primarily be consistent with long-range goals.

9. **Be sure your actions support your communications.** In the final analysis, the most persuasive communication is not what you say, but what you do. When actions contradict words, others tend to discount what you have said.

10. **Seek not only to be understood, but also to understand.** When one starts talking, they often cease to listen. Even more serious is the

occasional inattentiveness one may be guilty of when others are attempting to communicate with you. Listening is one of the most important, and most difficult, and most neglected skills in communication.

Key Negotiation Strategies

Negotiating is a process in which two or more parties communicate about an issue in dispute to reach an agreement. Most managers experience situations on the job in which they must negotiate with others, e.g. negotiating agreements with workers or other managers. In today's team-based organizations, where members are increasingly finding themselves having to work with colleagues over whom they have no direct authority and with whom they may not even share a common supervisor, negotiation skills become critical. In negotiating with others, managers should strive to reach an agreement which benefits both parties. While no two situations are ever exactly alike when negotiating, there are some key elements for effective negotiations. Negotiation depends significantly on effective communications to reach agreement. It also depends on establishing a clear goal to work toward, gathering sufficient and factual data and information to support your position, and understanding the other's goal, motivations, values, needs, and viewpoints. Understanding the other person's perspective and personal characteristics gives you valuable information that will assist you in negotiations. Seltz and Modica in their book **Negotiate Your Way to Success** present the following *key negotiating strategies:*

* **Keep it friendly.** Do not make negotiating an adversarial process with the other person as an enemy. Most of the job negotiations will be with workers with whom you must regularly work in the future and it's easier to get something from a friend. Winning the person over can produce long run benefits for you as a supervisor. Begin with a positive overture or small concession, since concessions tend to be reciprocated and lead to agreement.

* **Focus on each other's interests.** Interests exist before positions and emphasizing overall positions can lead to impasse or compromise without either parties interests being met.
Address problems and issues, not the personal characteristics of the other

party.

* **Bridge the gap.** When an impasse exists or parties are too far apart on an issue, do not give up, but bridge the gap by refocusing on new issues. This will not complicate matters, but give the parties more flexibility and more opportunities for trade-offs and agreement. Emphasize win-win and integrative solutions.

* **Negotiate from objective criteria.** Use independent and established standards to evaluate alternatives, so a wise, fair, and objective agreement can be reached with no one being taken advantage of.

* **Give a plausible reason.** Get the other party to accept your proposal or offer by always giving them a reason for doing so. Do not rely on the idea to sell itself or be readily known. Give a plausible reason for the other to accept your idea.

* **Differentiate to avoid setting an undesirable precedent.** Always differentiate your situation as unique with different variables to avoid a response from the other party that it will set an undesirable precedent.

* **Use a positive negotiating approach.** Show a positive spirit of cooperation and seek win-win outcomes. If you come on strong and abrasive, try to dictate conditions, and force someone to give in to your demands, resistance will be met. Keep an open mind, be flexible, and treat the other with respect and courtesy so it will be reciprocated. Be a good listener.

* **Establish a fail-safe point.** Set a line that separates the offers you will accept from the ones you will not accept in advance. To avoid getting caught up in the intensity of negotiations, know your minimum demands before negotiation begins.

* **Avoid questionable tactics.** Resorting to intentionally misleading statements, false data, and intimidation to take advantage of the other is unethical, although some do. While it may be marginally successful in the short run, the long-run benefit and damage to relationships and other issues will be significant. An individual's reputation as a fair, honest, and trustworthy supervisor can be greatly damaged.

Openness and Trust Model

Openness and trust builds healthy relationships that contribute to successful communication. Two researchers examined openness and trust and suggested that managers use their model to build open relationships and honest communication. The **Johari Window Model** by Joe Luft and Harry Ingham illustrates that there are certain things that a person knows about oneself and other things that one does not know about oneself. Similarly, there are things others do and do not know about that person. By reducing his or her "blind or hidden" areas, a manager can give himself or herself AND subordinates more and more accurate information. This leads to better perceptual processes, greater trust, and more honest communication. Likewise, subordinates can overcome perceptual and credibility weaknesses by engaging in increased self-disclosure and being more open and trusting.

Technological Factors in Communication

The Internet

The Internet is a global system of computer networks that are easy to join and are used by workers and managers of organizations around the world to communicate both inside and outside of organizations. It is estimated that about forty million people in the United States were on the Internet in 1997 and the rate of use is rapidly expanding. It is used to communicate with customers, vendors, and internally with workers. Some managers and organizations do not conduct many of their business transactions over the Internet because of security concerns. Only time will tell whether the Internet will be secure enough and if people will believe that it is secure enough for many transactions. The use of the Internet for electronic mail (e-mail) is rapidly expanding and has much potential for organizational use and benefit.

Some other recent, interesting observations about the Internet have been noted by the author:

- The California Governor budgeted $5 million for 1998 to bring California Virtual University on-line (500 courses at 65 colleges) (Wall Street Journal, 1/7/98)

- Lewis Perelman, technology and education author, sees no financial help for state-supported educational technology and advocates privatizing (Technos Quarterly, Fall 97)

- University professors in Canada have negotiated a new contract that ensures they will not be forced to use technology in the classroom if they don't want to (Chronicle of Higher Education, 10/30/97)

- A Central Florida Counseling group offers treatment for compulsive Internet users who withdraw from reality into a false cyberworld (AP, 01/04/98)

- Researchers find that the Internet has been expanding at a 200% annual rate for 10 years, doubling in size every 53 days (UCLA Institute for Cyberspace Law, 01/25/98)

These dramatic but somewhat paradoxical events represent reality and emphasize the inconsistency and contrasting views for the future of the Internet, heralded by some as the most important change in organizations and in telecommunications since the introduction of television in the late 1940's.

The Internet, popularly called the Net, was created in 1969 for the U.S. Department of Defense. Funding from the Advanced Research Projects Agency (ARPA) allowed researchers to experiment with methods for computers to communicate with each other. Their creation, the Advanced Research Projects Agency Network (ARPANET), linked only four separate computer sites at U.S. universities and research institutes, where it was used primarily by scientists. In the mid-1990s the appearance of the *World Wide Web* made the Internet even more popular. The Web is a multimedia interface that allows for the transmission of text, pictures, audio, and video together, known as Web pages, which commonly resemble pages in a magazine. Together these various elements have made the Internet a world- wide, higher education medium for communication, research, and for the retrieval of information on virtually any topic by organizations and individuals.

Cyberspace Law Considerations

The sudden growth of the Internet caught the legal system unprepared. Before 1996 there was little Federal legislation on this form of telecommunication. In 1986 Congress passed the Electronic Communication Privacy Act (ECPA) 18 U.S.C.A. 2701 et seq. [1996], which made it illegal to read private e-mail. The ECPA extended most of the protection already granted to conventional mail to electronic mail. Just as the post office may not read private letters, neither can the provider of private bulletin boards, on-line services, or Internet access. However, law enforcement agencies can subpoena e-mail in a criminal investigation. ECPA also permits employers to read their workers' e-mail. This provision was intended to protect companies against industrial spying, but has generated lawsuits from employees who objected to the invasion of their privacy. Federal courts, however, have allowed employers to secretly monitor an employee's e-mail on a company-owned computer system, concluding that employees have no reasonable expectation of privacy when they use company e-mail.

Computer Crime:

Criminal activity on the Internet generally falls into the category of computer crime. It includes so-called *"hacking"*, or unauthorized access to computer systems, including stealing account passwords and credit card numbers, and illegally copying intellectual property. Because personal computers can easily copy information--- including everything from software to photographs and books--- and the information can be sent to anywhere in the world quickly, it has become much more difficult for copyright owners in organizations education to protect their work.

The Internet has opportunities for workers, students and others to be involved in illegal adventures in computer crime. In particular, rebellious individuals may challenge authority through computer manipulations in cyberspace. In 1997, a young cyberthief hacker or *"cracker"* who was a computer programmer was arrested in North Carolina for using a personal computer and modem illegally. He commandeered a telephone company's digital, central office switch by dialing in remotely to acquire free calls, eavesdrop on key leaders, take over directory assistance and operator calls, and change the class of service on home phones to pay phone status. As a teenager, he destroyed files of a company, took passwords and combinations to door locks of several telephone company offices, obtained a copy of the operating system for a major computer company's research laboratory, and was caught using a university computer to gain illegal access to the Pentagon's Advanced Research Projects Agency network. He has been arrested many times, served time in several juvenile prisons, and agreed to one year in prison and a counseling program for his computer Internet "addiction". There is a reason to be aware of the possibilities of computer crime and breach of security in organizations.

American businesses lose more than $100 million yearly due to computer-related theft alone, e.g. the theft of ten million dollars from Citibank by Russian hackers in 1997, according to the San Francisco Chronicle in March of 1997. Certainly, educational institutions are not immune from computer crime and *spamming*. The very academic freedom concept which is indigenous to higher education may actually serve as a cultural catalyst to activities bordering on illegality. Thousands of "spammers" many of whom are suspected of being involved in fraudulent Internet schemes, have recently received letters from the Federal Trade Commission (FTC) Bureau of Consumer Protection warning them to clean up their act, according to USA Today, 2/6/98. The FTC is targeting people who send "spam" or unsolicited junk e-mail involving illegal chain letters, business opportunities that appear fraudulent, credit solicitations, and products making deceptive claims. If the spammers continue with their activities, the FTC can request court orders to stop marketers' activities and freeze their assets.

Electronic Mail (E-Mail):

As part of the revolution in high-tech communications, electronic mail, or e-mail, has soared in popularity with over 40 million U.S. citizens in 1997 regularly e-mailing each other by computer. Faster and cheaper that traditional mail, this correspondence is commonly sent over office networks, through national services and across the Internet. It is, however, less secure than traditional mail, even though Federal law protects e-mail from unauthorized tampering and interception. Under the Electronic Communications Privacy Act of 1986 (ECPA), third parties are forbidden to read private e-mail. However, a loophole in the ECPA that allows employers to read their workers' e-mail has provided especially controversial. This has provoked several lawsuits and produced legislative and extralegal proposals to increase e-mail privacy.

A 1997 survey by the Society for Human Resources Management shows that 86% of the 757 human resources professionals polled now use e-mail, but 49% of their companies don't train employees in the proper use of electronic messaging and 48% don't have written e-mail policies. Sixty-three percent say their firms do not officially allow personal use of the company e-mail system, but do nor monitor messages. Six percent had been asked to produce copies of e-mail messages as evidence for lawsuits, according to the Miami Herald newspaper, 1/12/98.

To protect against disclosure of private or sensitive information, some attorneys advise employers and employees to exercise caution with e-mail, since it can be subpoenaed. Some experts have advised users to delete their e-mail regularly, and even to avoid saving it in the first place. Still others advocate the use of encryption software, which scrambles messages and makes them unreadable without a digital password.

The vulnerability of e-mail messages goes far beyond access to stored files. Apart from potential problems with hackers or prying systems operators, some e-mail systems actually copy messages as they pass through the system. Other systems may automatically create back-up copies of new e-mail as it arrives on system "servers." Thus even erasing messages from in-boxes and out-boxes may not actually delete e-mail form system files. Attorneys have been amazed to discover that they can actually obtain access to electronic communication by relying on such automatic "storage" devices. From a legal perspective, too, e-mail users have substantially less protection in most jurisdictions today than those who converse on the telephone or send traditional mail through the U.S. Postal Service. And for most users of either the Internet or private electronic mail systems, determining the parameters of this protection is complex inquiry that is likely to trigger an analysis of wide-ranging and often contradictory body of law. To begin with, some privacy protections are available under the U.S. Constitution. These protections are typically rooted in the Fourth Amendment's guarantee against unreasonable searches and seizures and in the Fourth Amendment's implied right of privacy in the areas of marriage, procreation, contraception, and abortion.

Lawsuits regarding the nature and extent of e-mail privacy are beginning to make their way into the courts. Two recent California cases are particularly instructive in this regard. For example, in a class action lawsuit brought against Epson under California Penal Code Section 631, which provides a private cause of action for illegal interceptions of private wire communication, seven hundred employees argued that the company was illegally intercepting and reading e-mail messages on the office system. The trial court ruled in favor of Epson, however, declaring (1) that it was not clear that theses employees had a reasonable expectation of privacy in their e-mail messages, and (2) that even if plaintiffs had such an expectation, Section 631 did not apply to e-mail (Flanagan v. Epson America, Inc., 1991).

In a similar lawsuit filed under tort law by employees who argued that the Nissan Motor Company was tortuously intercepting many of their personal e-mail messages, the California Court of Appeal affirmed the trial court's decision that Nissan was well within its rights to do so. The court reasoned in a unpublished opinion that plaintiffs had no reasonable expectation of privacy because they had signed a waiver form which stated that "it is company policy that employees restrict their use of company-owned computer hardware and software to company business." (Bourke v. Nissan Motor Corp., 1993).

Cyberstalking:

On-line sexual harassment or *cybertalking* can occur in a wide variety of contexts, ranging from e-mail to chat rooms. Usenet groups, mailing lists, and home pages of organizational web sites have also been known to contain sexually explicit communication that may include unwelcome sexual advances, request for sexual favors, and other verbal conduct of a sexual nature.

In some cases this harassment may become a systematic campaign against you at work, where your harasser bombards you with threatening e-mail messages of hate and obscenity. As if this is not distressful enough, the situation can even escalate to the point where your harasser traces your work and home addresses and telephone numbers, and then you are facing not just emotional distress but also physical danger.

On-line stalking may be just as frightening and distressing as off-line stalking... and just as illegal. The fact is that both men and women have the same rights on-line as off-line, and NO ONE has a right to harass, threaten and distress you, especially in a work environment. On many networks and with many service providers, harassment of another user is a violation of their Acceptable Use Policy and abusers can have their accounts terminated. And in certain circumstances, once harassment becomes a systematic and malicious campaign of threats against you, then the harasser is breaking the law and there are a number of steps you can take to deal with it, both through the criminal and civil courts as appropriate. Both men and women can be stalked on-line, but the majority of the victims, as off-line, are female. It is estimated by the Cyberangels support group that 80% of stalking victims are female and that most cyberstalkers are male. Current estimates are that there are 200,000 real life stalkers in America today, out of a population of around 250 million. As regards stalking victims, it is estimated that over 1.5 million Americans today have been or are currently stalking victims, many in the work place.

THE PROCESS OF PLANNING EFFECTIVE GOALS AND OBJECTIVES

Importance of Planning

As was noted earlier, planning as one of the five principal functions of management, is a process that managers use to identify and select appropriate goals, objectives, and courses of action for their organization.

Planning is important because it is a useful way of getting managers involved in decision making about appropriate goals and strategies, gives the organization, managers, and workers a sense of purpose and direction, helps the communication and coordination among managers of diverse functions, and can be used as a motivating-controlling tool for getting commitment, measuring effective accomplishment of goals and performance.

Planning Steps

The *planning process* consists of three major steps: (1) determining an organization's (overall or unit) mission, vision, and major goals and objectives; (2) choosing strategies, or making the general decisions and taking the related actions and directions to attain them (e.g. formulating policies); and (3) selecting the appropriate manner of organizing resources to implement the strategies, including allocating specific responsibilities and resources to appropriate workers, units, and groups; drafting detailed action plans and procedures; and specifying how a strategy is to be specifically implemented (e.g. time horizons; measurable criteria). Certainly, planning should take place in all organizations. In large organizations, planning can take place at the total organization or corporate level, the division or business product/service level, and the department or functional level. Plans are developed for the long-term (usually five years or more), the intermediate-term (between one and five years), and the short-term (one year or less).

Types of Plans

There are at least five ways to classify plans: (1) *functional* area covered, such as human resources, marketing, finance, and production; (2) *organization level*, entire organization, unit, or subunit; (3) *characteristics* of the plans, e.g. costs involved, completeness, complexity, or formality; (4) *time* involved, such as short, intermediate, or long range; and (5) *activities*, including operations, personnel selection, advertising, research and development.

Another very general way to classify plans is (1) *strategic*; (2) *standing*; and (3) *single-use* plans. Strategic plans define the overall direction and fix the nature of the organization and include mission and vision plans. Standing plans remain fixed for long periods of time and include policies, procedures, and rules. Single-use plans include programs, projects, and budgets.

POLICIES: General statements of purpose, intent, and understandings that are guides to, or channels of, thinking and decision making by managers and workers; are standing plans; *broad guidelines.*

PROCEDURES: Establish a standard or routine method or technique of related actions that must be taken to accomplish a recurring task; they specify in detail how to proceed in all instances if some specific situation arises; are standing plans; *methods to carry out policies.*

RULES: Indicate what an organization member should or should not do under a given set of circumstances and allow NO room for interpretation; mandatory courses of action chosen from among available alternatives; are standing plans; designate *specific required action.*

PROGRAMS: A single-use plan designed to carry out a special project within an organization; a mixture of goals, objectives, strategies, policies, procedures, rules, and required resources; usually involves a long-term commitment of resources, but not intended to remain in existence over entire life of organization; exists to *achieve some purpose.*

PROJECT: Individual segments of a general program which are separate and distinct; a very *flexible*, single-use plan that adapts to a variety of situations; used where operations can be easily divided into separate parts with a clear termination point; usually *short-term* in nature.

BUDGETS: A detailed, single-use plan or forecast and guide for the financial results expected from an officially-recognized program of operations; serves both preventive planning AND corrective control roles; it covers a specified period of time and details *how funds will be spent* by area.

The Goal and Objective Setting Process

Goals Versus Objectives

Goals are general statements of intent that guide our overall direction, while objectives are specific desired, quantifiable and measurable outcomes that direct our actions. For example, our goal may be to satisfy our customers, but our objective is to provide quality service in terms of XYZ results without more than one complaint a month while providing service X at least ten times a month. Some use the terms goal and objective interchangeably. Certainly, supervisors are involved with setting and implementing goals and objectives. Both goals and objectives are a part of strategic planning, which consists of those activities leading

to the definition of the organization's mission and vision, the setting and prioritizing of fundamental objectives, and the development of strategies that enable it to function successfully. Strategic planning involves decisions made by top managers with significant long-term impact, ultimate allocation of large amounts of resources, and focuses on the organization's interaction with the external environment. While top managers establish overall organizational objectives, supervisors are concerned with unified objective setting for their work unit which serves as a basis for team and employee motivation and for performing the function of control.

Purposes of Objectives

Objectives serve four major purposes:

1) To define the role that the work unit plays relative to the total organization and environment.
2) To help supervisors and managers to coordinate their actions.
3) To provide a sense of direction and serve as guides for making and implementing decisions which promotes workers' identification with and loyalty to the organization.
4) To serve as performance standards against which actual performance may be checked.

The MBO Process

Management By Objectives (*MBO*) converts overall organizational objectives into specific objectives for organizational units and individual workers. It provides a process by which objectives cascade down through an organization and are mutually set and agreed upon by individuals and their managers. When in place, MBO creates a hierarchy of objectives that links objectives at one level to those at the next level. Performance reviews are conducted periodically to determine how close individuals are to attaining their objectives. Rewards are given to individuals on the basis of how close they come to reaching their goals.

Generally, the MBO process consists of these steps:

1). **Review organizational objectives.** The manager gains a clear understanding of the organization's overall goals and objectives.
2). **Set worker objectives.** The manager and worker meet to mutually agree on challenging worker objectives to be accomplished by the end of the normal operating period. Both quality and quantity dimensions of performance should be included. Realistic deadlines and priorities are specified for each objective to reduce ambiguity.
3). **Monitor progress.** At intervals during the normal operating period, the manager and worker check to see if the objectives are being reached. Frequent feedback mechanisms should be built in to assess objective

progress

4). **Evaluate performance.** At the end of the normal operating period, the worker's performance is judged by the extent to which thee worker accomplished the objectives.

5). **Give rewards.** Rewards are given to the worker based on the extent to which objectives are accomplished. The rewards should reflect objective difficulty, as well as objective outcomes.

Characteristics of Practical Objectives

Organizational objectives are practical guides for decision making, efficiency, consistency, and performance evaluation. Managers know the everyday direction in which the organization must move and it is their responsibility to make decisions that move the organization toward the achievement of objectives and especially short-run results. Managers must establish objectives that are <u>efficient</u> in terms of the total amount of human effort and resources their work unit uses to move toward attainment of objectives. Operational work unit objectives must be <u>consistent</u> and serve as a guide to encouraging productive activity, quality decisions, and effective planning. Objectives are the guidelines or criteria that should be used as the <u>basis for performance evaluations</u>. Those individuals who contribute most to attaining objectives should be considered the most productive.

Criteria for Verifiable Objectives

The following criteria are suggested for managers to follow for setting effective objectives:

1) **REALISTIC.** The objective should be practical and feasible for the work unit and not merely theoretical and idealistic. Will achieving the objective make a real contribution to your organization and its personnel? Set objectives for five or six key performance areas that really are important, rather than 15 objectives in non-critical areas, to focus attention.

2) **SPECIFIC AND PRECISE.** The objective statement must be definite as to precisely what you want to accomplish and specified in exact, quantitative terms, rather than vague and general terms, to minimize confusion and misunderstanding. It must include a measure against which results may be compared.

3) **ACHIEVABLE WITHIN DEFINITE TIME PERIOD.** The objective statement should include an attainable target date which allows for unforeseen contingencies. A deadline holds workers accountable over a period of time and allows for periodic assessment of their performances. Workers can then be flexible and pace themselves accordingly for results. Managers should set objectives high enough that workers will have to strive to meet them, but not so high that they will give up trying to meet them and become demoralized.

4) **CONSISTENT.** Key performance areas tend to be interrelated, so supervisors must consider the impact objectives have on one another, balance them so they do not overlap, and set them in relation to other work units to minimize *suboptimization,* when subobjectives are conflicting or not directly aimed at accomplishing overall organizational objectives. For example, one functional work area could consume too much of a resource so it would not be available for another functional area, hindering the latter unit's objective AND overall mission accomplishment.

5) **STATED AS END RESULTS.** Objectives should be stated in terms of what you ultimately want to accomplish or achieve, the actual end results, rather than in terms of ongoing processes and activities. For example, instead of "To increase awareness of the new maintenance system..." an objective could be stated "To reduce the frequency of repair on the XYZ aircraft by 10% within 6 months." Written objectives are better developed, document management expectations, provide a means for review, and minimize differences of opinion. Managers should relate objectives to specific required actions, to avoid worker inferences.

6) **VERIFIABLE.** A means for determining whether the objective has been accomplished by the target date should be established. Workers

should know exactly how supervisors will determine whether or not an objective has been reached. Managers should not wait until the end of the performance period to determine whether or not objectives are being met. Use intermediate progress or milestone checks and take appropriate follow up action.

Relevant Considerations for Setting Objectives

A practical understanding of various incidental circumstances and people concerns is necessary for setting and attaining objectives. There must be consideration of the mission, vision, elements to analyze, worker empowerment, and assumptions and limitations.

Mission and Vision Statements

Mission and vision statements are general goals and philosophical descriptions of the overall direction and major purpose of the organization. These statements are usually ideal in nature and provide a general sense of the "big picture" direction, the total organization's primary function, and what it hopes to achieve. A mission statement describes the main task faced by the organization, the medium in which it operates, and portrays a long-term goal.

The United States Air Force **Mission** is an excellent example of a mission statement:

"To defend the United States through control and exploitation of air and space."

A vision statement is a general picture of attaining the future organizational goal. It serves as a guiding visualization to point and confirm the organizational direction and to help organizational members focus on their purpose.

The United States Air Force **Vision** follows:

"Air Force people building the world's most respected air and space force... global power and reach for America."

Priorities

Priority of objectives means that at a given time accomplishing one objective is more important that accomplishing any of the others. It also reflects the relative importance of certain objectives, regardless of time. Certainly, managers must establish priorities if they want to allocate resources rationally and achieve success, but sometimes managers neglect to establish alternative objectives and evaluate and rank them. Determining priorities of objectives and justifying the rankings, especially to oneself, is inherently a judgmental decision by supervisors which is difficult, but must be done and done according to criteria.

SWOT Analysis   EXHIBIT # 4

Technique:

A useful planning technique for helping managers identify key internal and external factors affecting objectives, as well as identify potential organizational opportunities, is called SWOT analysis. SWOT is the process of systematically identifying an organization's strengths (S), weaknesses (W), opportunities (O), and threats (T). In essence, a manager would list the **strengths** and **weaknesses** of his or her work unit, in cooperation with work unit members. A consensus agreement on elements would be sought. Also, they would collectively list through the consensus process the **opportunities** and **threats** external to their work unit which could, respectively, help or hinder accomplishment of their objectives. This approach helps work unit members confront, define, and agree on a clearer picture of their unit's position for reaching objectives. After the listings and discussions, importance weights or probabilities can be assigned to each item to further assist with prioritizing and distinguishing urgent from important variables.

Typical SWOT Questions:

Potential strengths: Well-developed strategy? Broad market coverage? Good marketing skills? Human resource competencies? Appropriate management style?

Potential Opportunities: Expand core business? Diversify into new growth business? Widen product range? Apply R & D skills in new areas? Reduce rivalry among competitors? Overcome barriers to market entry?

Potential Weaknesses: Poorly developed strategy? Obsolete, narrow product lines? Growth without direction? Infighting among departments? High conflict and politics? Inadequate human resources?

Potential Threats: Increase in domestic competition? Potential for takeover? Downturn in economy? Slower market growth? Increase in foreign competition?

Employee Involvement and Empowerment

There is a reshaping of the relationship between managers and workers going on now. Managers are being called coaches, advisers, sponsors, and facilitators, while workers are now "associates" in some organizations. There is a blurring between the roles of managers and workers. In some organizations, decision making is being shared at certain levels and being pushed down to the operating level, where workers are being given the freedom and direct responsibility to make choices about procedures, schedules, and solving work-related problems, individually and in teams. The empowering manager's role is to show trust, provide vision, remove performance-blocking barriers, offer encouragement, and coach workers. Such world famous companies like General Electric, Intel, Ford, NCR, and Goodyear have introduced empowerment. Many have introduced empowerment as part of their efforts in implementing total quality management. Earlier, managers were encouraged to get their workers to "be involved" and to "participate." Generally, workers want to be involved in decisions that affect them, but should all workers be involved in all decisions and in all situations? A concern with the current empowerment movement is that it ignores the extent to which leadership and management can be shared and the conditions and situations facilitating success of shared leadership and management. It generally advocates an all-situation application, rather than a contingency and situational approach. While a consensus may not always be necessary, provisions for expressing views and sentiments do generate worker satisfaction and support for objectives. Now, certain organizations are going even further by allowing workers full control of their work and even where they do it, e.g. at home. *Self-managed teams*, where workers operate largely without supervisors, exist now. Some organizations are empowering workers to take control and be directly and totally accountable for what they do. Some managers are having to learn how to give up control and authority, while others are having to learn how to take responsibility for their work and make appropriate decisions. This *empowerment* concept is changing leadership styles, power relationships, the way work is designed, the way organizations are structured, the way objectives are set and achieved, and the job of the supervisor. Because of factors such as downsizing, higher worker skills, implementation of total quality management programs, and introduction of self-managed teams, an increasing number of situations call for a more empowering approach to management and leadership, but not ALL situations.

Assumptions and Limitations

Situations temper objectives, resources, and management styles, but it seems that every manager always wants more resources, i.e. more people, more equipment, or more funds. When managers set objectives and plan their implementation, they should know existing as well as potential limits. If a manager does not judge their current situation realistically, they will be frustrated when upper management does not support their additional resource requests. Managers should be careful of their assumptions and recognize overall limitations.

THE DELEGATION OF AUTHORITY PROCESS

Delegation Philosophy and Attitude

Delegation is the process by which managers assign job activities and authority downward to specific workers within their work unit and establish responsibility for how authority is used. It is important that delegation of authority and responsibility go together. There are many reasons managers fail to delegate tasks and authority to others. Some fail to delegate because they find using their authority very satisfying. Also, they may get such a high level of intrinsic satisfaction from the hands-on work that they do not want to relinquish the activity, even though they have other managerial work to perform. Managers may fear that their workers will not do a job well or that surrendering some of their authority may be seen by others as a sign of weakness. Also, if managers are insecure in their jobs or see specific activities as being extremely important to their personal success, they may not want to give the performance of these activities to others. Even if managers wish to delegate, they may find several subordinate-related roadblocks. Workers may be reluctant to accept delegated authority for fear of failure or because of a lack of self-confidence. Characteristics of the organization itself may make delegation difficult, e.g. a small work unit may present the manager with only a minimal number of activities to be delegated.

Steps in the Delegation Process

The following summarizes the primary steps involved in delegation:

1) **CLARIFY THE ASSIGNMENT.** Begin with determining what is to be delegated and to whom. The supervisor needs to identify the worker best capable of doing the task, then determine if he or she has time and is willing to do it. It is very important to provide clear instructions and information on what is being delegated, the expected results, and the time deadlines. Whenever possible, the results should be stated in operational terms so that the worker knows exactly what action must be taken to perform the assigned duties. Unless there is a specific requirement to adhere to specific methods, the supervisor should delegate only the end results, letting the worker decide on the means.

2) **GRANT AUTHORITY.** Appropriate authority must be given, so the worker will have the right and power within the organization to accomplish the assigned duties. Every act of delegation comes with constraints, since the supervisor is not granting unlimited authority, but specific authority to act on certain issues within certain parameters. Specify those parameters so workers know, without question, the range of their power.

3) **ALLOW WORKER PARTICIPATION.** The worker is the best source for determining how much authority is appropriate to accomplish a task. By allowing the worker a chance to be involved in determining how much authority is needed to get the job done and the standards by which they will be evaluated, the manager can increase their motivation, satisfaction, and accountability for performance. Everything should not be delegated, since some duties are the manager's alone, e.g. technical knowledge that only you possess or confidential information or actions. This step confirms worker acceptance of the delegation and thus creates an obligation and responsibility.

4) **INFORM OTHERS.** Delegation should not take place only within that single work unit. Not only does the manager and worker need to

know specifically what has been delegated and how much authority has been granted, but anyone else who may be affected by the delegation act also needs to be informed. Put all delegations in writing and distribute it to appropriate individuals.

5) **ESTABLISH CONTROLS.** The establishment of controls to monitor the worker's progress increases the likelihood that key problems will be identified and that the task will be completed on time and according to specifications. The manager should set progress check dates when the worker reports back on how well he is doing and any problems that have arisen. Spot checks may be necessary to ensure authority is not being abused and that policies and procedures are being followed.

Key Considerations in Successful Delegation

Objective Specificity

Managers must specify and clearly define the tasks being delegated, as well as those not being delegated. When workers are given an assignment, they should know exactly what their authority and responsibility is and what is expected of them. In addition, managers should provide information about how their assignment fits into the overall scheme of things. Managers should make clear the extent of support and direction those delegated to do the job may expect, especially from their manager. The workers should know who they can go to for additional information, when they should come to you with problems, and whom they should not approach.

Objective Difficulty

Edwin Locke proposed that intentions to work toward a goal are a major source of work motivation. His work supports the conclusions that specific objectives increase performance, that difficult objectives, when accepted, result in higher performance than do easy ones, and that feedback leads to higher performance than does non-feedback. The specificity of the objective itself acts as an internal stimulus. If factors like ability and acceptance of goals are held constant, managers can expect that the more difficult an objective, the higher the level of worker performance will be. However, it's logical to assume that easier objectives are more likely to be accepted. Once a worker accepts a hard task, he or she will exert a high level of effort until it is achieved or abandoned. The **lesson for managers** is clear: For higher levels of job performance, *set specific and realistic but challenging objectives*, since easy goals will result in lower performance.

Feedback

In line with Locke's research, to get people to do their best managers should *provide workers with feedback* about the results of their performance in relation to the difficult objective. Feedback helps identify discrepancies between what they have done and what they want to do; it guides behavior. Interestingly, all feedback is not equally potent. Ivancevich and McMahon report in the Academy of Management Journal that self-generated feedback (where the worker is able to monitor his or her own progress) has been shown to be a more powerful motivator than externally-generated feedback.

Participation

Why should workers participate in delegation and accept a delegated job and more work? Managers should know that the reasons for accepting the delegated work are:

* Workers get a chance to learn and a bigger picture of the work unit.
* Workers get more of a variety of tasks and different things to do, which provides more job satisfaction.
* Delegation is a reward for other work well done and satisfies an ego need.

Overcoming Obstacles to Effective Delegation

Acceptance

Acceptance of the need to delegate is a major obstacle for managers. Other barriers to effective delegation can be present in the manager, the subordinate workers, and the situation. Most managers recognize the primary advantage of delegation, which is spreading the work among a larger number of workers, helps managers become less harried and more effective. Delegation can free supervisors from making numerous routine or minor decisions, so they can devote more time to broader and more complex decisions. **The biggest obstacle to delegation is the manager not accepting that he or she should delegate routine tasks.** Managers must show confidence in workers, not fear competition from them, and overcome the belief that "if you want it done right, you must do it yourself." Also, the false philosophy that being busy with many routine tasks is the same as being productive must be overcome.

Common Barriers

The barriers or obstacles for the subordinates include a lack of self confidence, a desire to avoid responsibility, a real lack of job skills, and a lack of understanding of policies and procedures. The **manager must train and develop workers** and help them overcome these obstacles and perform the delegated tasks. The situational barriers include: the manager's boss may discourage delegation; there is need for a quick action; understaffing; and an organizational culture which discourages mistakes. Some of these are beyond the control of the manager and must be recognized.

Checklist for Effective Delegation

The following effective delegation checklist is offered as a guide for managers by Dale McConkey and the American Management Association:

1) Is there a written record for the delegation?
2) Did the worker participate in establishing the authority for the delegation and the expected standards of performance?
3) Is the delegated authority equal to the responsibility?
4) Can the worker plan ahead to accomplish his/her accountability with the knowledge that they have the requisite authority to accomplish the task?
5) Can the worker act to accomplish the task without fear of exceeding his/her authority or having their actions reversed by higher authority?
6) Do the supervisor's superiors, subordinates, and peers know of the delegation and authority granted?
7) Has an adequate control and feedback system been established to measure the effectiveness of the accomplishment of the delegated task and about how authority is being carried out?

THE MOTIVATION PROCESS AND HUMAN BEHAVIOR

The Complex Motivation Process

The Concept

Motivation is a subject about which there is very little agreement and common understanding and which has a lack of universally-accepted definitions and principles, because of its complexity. It explains why people behave the way they do and exert effort on the job. Since one of the important duties of a manager is to direct workers in such a manner that they are willing to exert sufficient, and frequently great, effort in applying their skills on the job for organizational success, **the motivation process is critical for managers.** Some of the managerial challenges include (1) identifying the differing needs and behaviors of various individuals, (2) creating a positive work environment and climate that encourages appropriate job effort and performance, (3) providing both intrinsic and extrinsic rewards and incentives for different workers, (4) assessing when workers' dissatisfactions and expectancies may lead to negative actions, and (5) knowing how to address those unique dissatisfactions and expectancies. If the manager can understand worker behavior, he or she can better predict it; if the manager can predict behavior, then he or she can better control it.

The author defines **motivation** in the workplace as the individual worker's willingness to exert high levels of effort toward organizational goals, which is conditioned by the effort's ability to satisfy individual needs and by the influence of external factors. This definition emphasizes six key elements: (1) individual effort, (2) willingness (desire), (3) goals, (4) ability, (5) needs, and (6) external factors (incentives). The following basic assumptions about human behavior and motivation are made: *MOTIVATION AND HUMAN BEHAVIOR ARE CAUSED, GOAL DIRECTED, AND DO NOT OCCUR IN ISOLATION.* In essence, a worker's behavior may be caused by the way they perceive the world, is directed toward achieving a certain goal, and results in individual motivation to achieve that goal. So on the job, the motivation process is basically one of cause and effect. Needs (motives) cause an inner willingness (desire) to overcome some lack or imbalance in the workplace. Stimuli (managerial incentives or rewards) are then applied to cause a worker to respond and behave, so that performance results. Thus, the goal of satisfying the worker's needs is achieved, and the organization achieves its desired output.

Internal Versus External Influences on Behavior

Although supervisors, managers, teachers, and others can create a climate of positive motivation, in the final analysis **MOTIVATION COMES FROM WITHIN EACH INDIVIDUAL.** The motivation process and elements described above are oversimplified, for a worker's ability, desire, and motivation are the result of many internal and external factors.

Certainly, the worker must have the ability or capacity to do the job. Sometimes this takes the form of physical dexterity, such as good hand-eye coordination. Someone who lacks this dexterity will never do well as a typist, no matter how much the person wants to succeed in this job. However, a worker may have the ability to do the job well, but also need proper training or education for developing that ability and overcoming job mistakes. This is a significant role for the manager. While ability is important, the desire and willingness to do the best possible job is probably more important. Without this drive for excellence, ability is of limited value. Of course, the manager plays an important role in building this desire through rewards and incentives.

While a worker's ability to perform the job is influenced by his or her learning and hereditary variables, motivation is influenced by several internal needs and expectancies and various external incentives. Worker expectancies include the individual's self concept, their perceptions about their environment, their cognitive learning style, and their aspirations. Incentives include supervisory, work group, financial, job content, promotional, physical, contextual, and environmental rewards and opportunities. Other organizational variables influence the motivation process and job performance, including job design, span of control, technology, group affiliations, and the manager's style. These factors form the basis for the motivation models which follow later.

Attitudes and Job Satisfaction

Attitudes affect, and may significantly influence, behavior and job satisfaction which are directed at performance and accomplishing job goals. Managers must understand attitudes and satisfaction and their relationship to motivation and goal achievement. Attitudes are evaluative statements about people, things, and events. They reflect how one feels about something and are not the same as values, but they are related. An attitude has three elements: cognitive, affective, and behavioral. Opinions and beliefs are cognitive components of attitudes concerned with thought processes, logic, and consciously acquiring and forming knowledge, while emotions and feelings (likes and dislikes) are the subjective affective components which can lead to behavioral outcomes. The behavioral element of an attitude refers to an intention to behave in a certain way toward someone or something. The affective or emotional element largely determines an attitude, so attitudes are less stable than values. While it is generally recognized that values do not have a direct impact on behavior, values strongly influence a worker's attitudes, so knowledge of a worker's value system can provide insight into his or her attitudes. In organizations, attitudes are important because they directly affect job behavior in a significant manner.

Job Satisfaction is a worker's general attitude toward his or her job. It is the worker's fulfillment acquired by experiencing various job activities and rewards from past performance. It is a complex summary of a number of previous, discrete job elements. Motivation and satisfaction are related, but not synonymous concepts. While motivation is primarily concerned with goal-directed behavior, satisfaction is a positive or negative attitude about the job. Both are need related. A manager's interest in job satisfaction must center on worker performance and the impact of job satisfaction on output, efficiency, productivity, development, absenteeism, turnover, and other elements of "effectiveness." Managers must consider the correlation between job satisfaction and high performance for the individuals in their particular work group, given the interactions and complexities of work processes and specific situations.

The Hawthorne Effect

Three researchers, Elton Mayo, F. Roethlisberger, and W. Dickson conducted studies at the Hawthorne plant of the Western Electric Company in Cicero, Illinois to discover the best work environment for job performance, to make workers more efficient and less tired. They felt is was important to evaluate the attitudes and reactions of workers to their jobs and their environment. These classic studies originally began in 1924, and extended through the early 1930s, to initially examine the effects of illumination levels on worker productivity. As the lights were turned up or down, worker productivity increased, so the researchers concluded that some **factors other than light were responsible for the increased productivity**. The relay assembly test room experiments were next where workers were subjected to various work conditions. About 20,000 interviews were conducted and workers were asked about the company, the environment, the type of supervisors, and their interpersonal relationships. The researchers realized that people were not at work simply for economic reasons and that **other human factors affected their job performance**. The subjects found working in the test room enjoyable, the supervisory relationship allowed them to work freely without fear, and subjects realized they were taking part in an important study. The final experiment was a bank wiring room experiment where the researchers discovered that the production quota set by the company was not the number of units actually produced by the workers, but that the workers determined their own level of output that was fair, a "norm" which was enforced by the group, e.g. if a worker produced more than the group norm, he was pressured by co-workers to comply with the norm. It was concluded that social norms or the **group standards were key determinants of individual work behavior**. The series of studies at the Hawthorne plant led to a new emphasis on the human factor and the need to understand people as individuals and as a member of a social group.

Behavior Modification and Reinforcement

A strategy that manager's can use in motivating workers is based primarily on a concept known as behavior modification, as advanced by B.F. Skinner. He defines it as encouraging appropriate behavior as a result of the consequences of that behavior. Behavior that is rewarded tends to be repeated, while behavior that is punished tends to be eliminated. Although behavioral modification programs involve the administration of both rewards and punishments, the rewards are generally emphasized since they have more effective influence on behavior than punishments. In essence, behavior modification asserts that if supervisors want to modify workers' behavior, they must ensure that appropriate consequences occur as a result of that behavior. With this approach, positive reinforcement and negative reinforcement are BOTH rewards that increase the likelihood that behavior will continue.

Positive reinforcement is a desirable consequence of a behavior, e.g. if a worker who arrives on time is positively reinforced (rewarded), the probability increases that he will be on time with greater frequency.

Negative reinforcement is the elimination of an undesirable consequence of behavior, e.g. if the worker experiences some undesirable outcome related to arriving to work late, such as a verbal reprimand, the worker is negatively reinforced when this outcome is eliminated, due to the worker arriving on time.

Behavior modification programs have been applied both successfully and unsuccessfully in many different organization. The behavior modification efforts at Emery Air Freight Company (now part of Federal Express) resulted in the conclusion that the establishment and use of an effective feedback system is very important in making a behavior modification program successful.

The Role of Values in Explaining and Predicting Behavior

Definition of Values

Our values are basic convictions that a specific type of conduct or outcome is personally or socially preferable to an opposite conduct or outcome, e.g. freedom, honesty, and self-respect.. They contain a judgmental component in that they contain an individual's personal ideas about what is good or bad, right or wrong, or desirable or undesirable. Values have both content and intensity characteristics in that they imply what conduct or outcome is IMPORTANT and HOW IMPORTANT it is. When we recognize and rank a worker's values, we obtain that worker's value system.

Allport's Types of Values

One of the early researchers to study and categorize values was Allport and his associates. They defined six types of values:

1) **THEORETICAL**: High importance on the discovery of truth through a critical analytical and rational approach
2) **ECONOMIC**: Emphasizes the useful and practical
3) **AESTHETIC**: High importance on form, appearance, and harmony
4) **SOCIAL**: Highest value on associating with others, belonging, and love of people
5) **POLITICAL**: Emphasizes the acquisition of power and influence
6) **RELIGIOUS**: High importance on the unity of experience and spiritual understanding of the cosmos as a whole.

Allport administered a questionnaire that described many different situations and asked respondents to preference-rank a fixed set of answers, so he could rank them in terms of importance relative to his 6 value types and identify a value system for each individual. He found that people in different occupations place different importance on his six value types. While the disadvantages of stereotyping are apparent, the values categorization approach may be helpful to supervisors as one factor to consider in understanding worker priorities, behaviors, and for translating ork decisions and job assignments.

EXHIBIT # 5

Dominant Values in Today's Work Force

Cherrington and associates offer the following model that shows the dominant values in today's work force by age and values of the worker:

WORK FORCE VALUES

STAGE	ENTERED WORK FORCE	WORK VALUES
Protestant Work Ethic	Mid 1940s to late 1950s	Hard Work Conservative Loyalty to Organization
Existential	1960s to Mid 1970s	Quality of Life Nonconforming Seeks Autonomy Loyal to Self
Pragmatic	Mid 1970s to late 1980s	Success; Ambition; Achievement; Hard Work; Loyalty to Career
Generation X	1990 to Present	Flexibility; Job Satisfaction; Leisure Time; Loyal to Relationships

EXHIBIT # 6

A Core Values Model

The United States Air Force's Core Values serve as an excellent example:

THE UNITED STATES AIR FORCE'S CORE VALUES

I. The Importance of Core Values

It is important for all Air Force personnel to regularly recognize, understand, and practice the basic Core Values, which are the fundamental standards and the ethical guides for our decision making and behavior. They remind us what it takes to get the mission done. They reflect the worth of who our Air Force people are and what they do, and serve as a psychic reward to us. They are important because they are a means for establishing trust among Air Force people who have to work very hard together in difficult and fast-paced circumstances. The Core Values are a set of critical ideals for the Air Force and for the way it presents to the American people who it is and to what it is committed. Most effective institutions in our society, whether private or public, are values based and have vision or mission statements that line up their values with their goals. The Core Values serve as a useful prism to examine any institution and help individuals sort out their options and make worthwhile commitments. It is essential that our Core Values be continually articulated and reinforced, since they set the standard for our behavior, our service to country, and our treatment of one another. The Core Values should remind us of our profession, the oath we have taken, and the demands placed upon us. Meeting these demands places us in a special category that deserves recognition and commendation. It allows us to place before the American people and their elected representatives the commitment that members of our services have made to the defense of our Nation and to their Commander-in-Chief.

II. The Three Core Values

Integrity First

Integrity is the willingness to do what is right, even when it is not convenient or comfortable to do so. It is the essential inner voice, the source of self control, and the basis for the trust that is imperative in today's military. It is doing the right thing when nobody's looking. It is the ability to hold together and properly regulate all of the elements of a personality. In this world of "me first" and relative ethics, honesty is still the hallmark of the military professional. It implies wholeness, an internal consistence. Subsumed within the core value of integrity are ideals such as honesty, courage, accountability, responsibility, justice, openness, self-respect, and humility. The nation expects honesty, as well as all of these moral traits, from us and we must always deliver. Our word and our high-level behavior must be our bond. We must not lose our ethical compass when we find ourselves in situations between our ambitions and our ideals. We must know the right things to do and have the moral fortitude to do them. We must be courageous in standing by our convictions and accept the responsibility to do the right things, rather than what is convenient, familiar, or popular.

Service Before Self

Service before self means that professional duties and the needs of our country take precedence over personal concerns and desires. As practitioners of the profession of arms, Air Force personnel serve as guardians of America's future and are entrusted with the security of our nation, the protection of its citizens, and the preservation of its way of life. We freely promise to support and defend the Constitution of the United States against all enemies, foreign and domestic, thus committing our lives in defense of America if necessary. By voluntarily serving in the military profession, we accept unique responsibilities which require a high degree of skill and a willingness to make personal sacrifices. At the very least it includes following rules, respecting others, discipline and self-control, and keeping faith in the system. Service before self is crucial for the Air Force and the nation.

Excellence In All You Do

Just getting by is an infectious attitude that can lead to mediocrity. Air Force personnel cannot let that happen. To perform our jobs optimally, we have to be motivated above the usual to a higher goal and be committed to achieving our full potentials. We must propel our drive for excellence in everything we do. We must develop a sustained passion for continuous improvement and innovation that will propel the Air Force into a long-term, upward spiral of accomplishment and performance. There is a personal satisfaction of performing at the very best level, at the very best of our abilities, that guarantees success. Truly effective professionals seize the problems and challenges as opportunities and motivate themselves and others to excel. This passion for excellence sets apart the significant from the superficial and the lasting from the temporary. Those who strive for excellence do so because of what is in them, not because of what others think or say or do. The superior person does not mind failing to get recognition, since he is too busy doing the excellent things that entitle him to the recognition. While a commitment to excellence is neither popular nor easy at times, it is essential. This means providing services and generating products that fully respond to customer wants and needs, being focused on personal and community excellence, and effectively managing resources. Our nation needs Air Force members performing at the very best of their abilities all the time, both in internal and external operations. We should not just drift along with the tide, but soar to new heights above the ordinary.

III. Assumptions About the Air Force Core Values Strategy

Assumptions

The following important assumptions govern the Core Values Strategy, according to the January, 1997 United States Air Force Core Values little blue book:

1. The Core Values Strategy exists independently of and does not compete with Chapel programs, i.e. all of us, regardless of our religious views, must recognize and accept the values;
2. You don't need to be a commander in order to be a leader;
3. The leader of an organization is key to its moral climate, i.e. as does the commander, so does the organization;
4. Leaders cannot just be good; they also must be sensitive to their status as role models for their people and thus avoid the appearance of improper behavior;
5. Leadership from below is at least as important as leadership from above in implementing the Core Values;
6. A culture of conscience is impossible unless civilians, officers, and enlisted personnel understand, accept, internalize, and are free to follow the Core Values;
7. To understand, accept, and internalize the Core Values, our people must be allowed and encouraged to engage in an extended dialogue about them and to explore the role of the values at all levels of the Air Force; and
8. Our first task is to fix organizations; individual character development is possible, but it is not a goal.

Operationalizing the Core Values as an integral part of the way we conduct our daily business requires a top-down implementation from leaders at all levels, a bottom-up analysis to examine and identify problems and actions, and a back-and-forth dialogue by all members as to how best to inculcate the Core Values into our organizational culture.

Values in Successful Organizations

In 1990, Francis and Woodcock conducted an organizational values study, identified specific values in several successful companies, and suggest the "active and persistent pursuit" of the following twelve values:

- **Power.** Managers must take charge and manage.

- **Elitism.** Get the best candidates into management jobs and continuously develop their competence.

- **Reward.** Identify and reward performance.

- **Effectiveness.** Focus resources on activities that get results.

- **Efficiency.** Relentlessly search for better ways to do things; do the right things.

- **Economy.** Face the importance of economic reality and economize; no free lunches.

- **Fairness.** Care about people; realize that people's views, perceptions, and feelings are important.

- **Teamwork.** Pull together and ensure the organization derives the benefit.

- **Law and Order.** Honorably administer an appropriate system of rules and regulations; justice must prevail.

- **Defense.** Study external threats and formulate a strong defense.

- **Competitiveness.** Take all necessary steps to be competitive; survival of the fittest.

- **Opportunism.** Seize opportunities quickly, even though there are risks; organizations should be committed opportunists.

Total Quality Management

Total quality management (TQM) programs are organization-wide programs that aim to integrate all functions of the business so that all functions are aimed at maximizing customer satisfaction through continuous process improvements and responding to customer needs and expectations. W. Edwards Deming is generally regarded as the intellectual father of total quality management. His TQM program is based on a 14-point system, which he says must be integrated at all organizational levels. See EXHIBIT # 7 for Deming's 14 TQM points.

EXHIBIT # 7

Deming's 14 TQM Points:

1). Create and publish to all employees a statement of the aims and purposes of the organization. Management must constantly demonstrate its commitment to this statement.
2). Learn the new philosophy; top management and everybody else.
3). Understand the purpose of inspection... for improvement of processes and reduction of cost.
4). End the practice of awarding business on the basis of price tag alone.
5). Improve constantly and forever the system of production and service.
6). Institute training.
7). Teach and institute leadership.
8). Drive out fear. Create trust. Create a climate for innovation.
9). Optimize the efforts of teams, groups, staff areas toward the aims and purposes of the company.
10). Eliminate exhortations to the workforce.
11). (a) Eliminate numerical quotas for production; instead learn and institute methods for improvement.
    (b) Eliminate management by objectives; instead learn the capabilities of processes and how to improve them.
12). Remove barriers that rob people of pride of workmanship.
13). Encourage education and self-improvement for everyone.
14). Take action to accomplish the transformation.

TQM Elements:

The following are the basic elements of any TQM system:

1). **Intense Customer Focus.** Focus on what customers want, not what management think they need.
2). **Emphasize Continuous Improvement.** Maintaining the status quo or even meeting specifications isn't enough, since many competitors are striving to beat performance and improve results. Continuously strive to

improve quality of products, services, and processes.
3). **Seek Problem Root Causes, Rather Than Symptoms.** Eliminate the key problem, so resources will not be repeatedly wasted addressing partial elements of the problem or symptoms.
4). **Focus On The Customer, Not Your Own Organization.** Change your paradigm and focus primarily on identifying and meeting the customer's needs, not your natural tendency to focus on what your organization does best and its needs, special skills, and procedures.

Needs and Their Implications for Performance

Needs Assessment Exercise   EXHIBIT # 8

The following Motivation-Needs Quiz from John Ivancevich and Associates is designed to assess the relative strength of each of an individual's major needs, based on the 5 need categories in Maslow's Hierarchy of Needs. After honestly completing and scoring the Quiz, an individual can understand the needs' categories that primarily motivate him or her.

MOTIVATION-NEEDS QUIZ

Directions: The following statements have 7 possible responses:

Strongly Agree	Agree	Slightly Agree	Don't Know	Slightly Disagree	Disagree	Strongly Disagree
+3	+2	+1	0	-1	-2	-3

Please number from 1 to 20 on a piece of paper and put the + or - number corresponding to the above response that matches your opinion. For example, if you "Strongly Agree," write the number "+3." Complete all 20 questions.

1. Special wage increases should be given to workers who do their jobs very well.

2. Better job descriptions would help workers to know exactly what is expected of them.

3. Workers need to be reminded that their jobs are dependent on the organization's ability to compete effectively.

4. A supervisor should give a good deal of attention to the physical working conditions of his workers.

5. The supervisor ought to strive to develop a friendly working atmosphere among her people.

6. Individual recognition for above-standard performance means a lot to workers.

7. Indifferent supervision can often bruise feelings.

8. Workers want to feel that their real skills and capacities are put to use on their jobs.

9. The organization retirement, benefits, and stock programs are important factors in keeping workers on their jobs.

10. Almost every job can be made more stimulating and challenging.

11. Many workers want to give their best in everything they do.

12. Management could show more interest in the employees by sponsoring after-hours social events.

13. Pride in one's work is actually an important reward.

14. Workers want to be able to think of themselves as "the best" at their own jobs.

15. The quality of the relationships in the informal work group is quite important.

16. Individual incentive bonuses would improve the performance of workers.

17. Visibility with upper management is important to workers.

18. Workers generally like to schedule their own work and to make job-related decisions with a minimum of supervision.

19. Job security is important to workers.

20. Having good equipment to work with is important to employees.

SCORING THE MOTIVATION-NEEDS QUIZ

1. Transfer the 20 numbers you listed in the Motivation-Needs Quiz to the appropriate places in the chart below.

Statement Number	Score	Statement Number	Score	Statement Number	Score
10		2		6	
11		3		8	
13		9		14	
18		19		17	

Total, Self-Actualization: Total, Safety: Total, Esteem:

CONTINUED NEXT PAGE

Statement Number	Score	Statement Number	Score
1		5	
4		7	
16		12	
20		15	

Total, Physiological: _____   Total, Social: _____

2. Record your total scores in the chart below by marking an X in each row next to the number of your total score for that area of needs motivation, so you can better visualize your scores.

```
              -12  -10  -8  -6  -4  -2  0  +2  +4  +6  +8  +10  +12
```

Self
Actualization

Esteem

Social

Safety

Physiological

          LOW USE   HIGH USE

Once you have completed this chart you can see the relative strength of each of these needs. Which need is your most deficient? Why? How do you plan to satisfy this need?

Maslow's Need Hierarchy

Probably the most well know theory of motivation is Abraham Maslow's Hierarchy of Needs. He hypothesized that within every human being there exists a hierarchy of the following five needs:

1. **PHYSIOLOGICAL**: Includes hunger, thirst, shelter, sex and other bodily needs.
Applied: Pay, vacation, holidays, lunch breaks, rest rooms, clean air to breathe
2. **SAFETY**: Includes security and protection from physical and emotional harm.
Applied: Safe working conditions, seniority plans, union, savings plans, pension vesting, medical and dental insurance plans, grievance system
3. **SOCIAL**: Includes belongingness, acceptance, love, affection, friendship
Applied: Formal and informal work groups, organization-sponsored activities, professional, civic, and social associations, a loving spouse
4. **ESTEEM**: Includes self-respect, status, autonomy, achievement, recognition, appreciation
Applied: Power, titles, status symbols, ego, recognition, praise, promotion, awards
5. **SELF-ACTUALIZATION**: Becoming what one is capable of becoming, growth, self-fulfillment
Applied: Completing challenging assignments, doing creative work, developing skills, being all that one is capable of being

Maslow believed that human needs are arranged in a hierarchy of prepotence where the needs at a particular level of the hierarchy must be relatively satisfied before the needs at the next higher level become a concern. Once a need is fairly-well satisfied in each individual's own terms, then it ceases to motivate behavior and the next higher level of needs becomes prepotent in motivating behavior. Maslow believed that only needs that are relatively unsatisfied are capable of motivating people and that behavior is complex and cannot be explained simplistically in terms of satisfying only one level of needs. An interesting study of military commanders by Mitchell supports this conclusion by Maslow. It found that higher-ranking military officers experience greater need satisfaction than do lower-ranking officers, except in social need satisfaction.

Alderfer's ERG Model

Clayton Alderfer has reworked Maslow's theory to align it more closely with empirical research and called it the ERG Theory. Alderfer presents three groups of core needs: existence (E), relatedness (R), and growth (G). Existence is concerned with providing our basic material existence requirements or Maslow's physiological and safety needs. Relatedness needs are the desires we have for maintaining important interpersonal relationships and align with Maslow's social need and the external component of Maslow's esteem classification. The growth needs are an intrinsic desire for personal development and include Maslow's esteem and self-actualization needs. In contrast to the hierarchy of needs, the ERG Theory demonstrates that more than one need may be operative at the same time and if the gratification of a higher level need is stifled, the desire to satisfy a lower level need increases (regression). While Maslow's hierarchy is a rigid steplike progression, ERG does not assume a rigid hierarchy where a lower need must be substantially gratified before one can move on, i.e. all three need categories can be operating at the same time. Some *propositions of ERG Theory* are:

1) The more the satisfaction of E needs is frustrated, the more E needs will be desired.
2) The more E needs are satisfied, the more R needs will be desired.
3) The more the satisfaction of R needs is frustrated, the more both E and R needs are desired.
4) The more R needs are satisfied, the more G needs will be desired.
5) The more the satisfaction of G needs is frustrated, the more R needs

will be desired.
6) The more G needs are satisfied, the more G needs will be desired.

McClelland's Three-Needs

Another theory of motivation which uses needs as the central focus is David McClelland's theory. It states that a major factor in willingness to perform is the intensity of the individual's need for **achievement**, the need for **power**, and the need for **affiliation**. Thus, McClelland's Three-Needs Theory. He defines achievement as the drive to excel and to succeed, power as the need to gain a position of status and authority and make others behave in a way they would not have behaved otherwise, and affiliation as the desire for friendly and close interpersonal relationships. McClelland found that workers with a *high need for achievement* have the following characteristics:

1. They like to take personal responsibility for finding solutions to problems.
2. They like to take calculated risks and set moderate goals, not too easy and not too difficult.
3. They like concrete feedback.

Useful Conclusions About Needs

There are some useful, and controversial, conclusions about needs by the needs theorists that managers should consider. **Maslow** concluded that when a need is basically satisfied, it is no longer a primary motivator, so satisfied needs no longer motivate. He also concluded that a higher-order need (social, esteem or self-actualization) cannot become an active motivating force until the preceding lower-order need (physiological or safety) is essentially satisfied. While he said needs are mutually exclusive, others believe that several needs can exist simultaneously. Finally, he concluded people seek growth and want to move up the hierarchy and self-actualization is the common climax to personal growth. However, this assumption may be true for some, but inaccurate for others. **Alderfer** concluded, in contrast, that multiple needs can be operating at the same time and that if a higher level need cannot be satisfied, gratification of a lower level need will be sought. Multiple variables, such as education, family background, and cultural factors, can alter the driving force of a group of needs for an individual. **McClelland** concludes that the motivation of high-need achievers is a function of the nature of the task responsibilities, the attainability of the task goals, and the regularity of feedback. Job success can be attained through power, friendship, or task achievement and supervisors must identify those paths and see that the behaviors workers display in taking them produces useful contributions.

<u>**Motivation Models**</u>

McGregor's Theory X and Y

Another aspect of motivation involves a supervisor's assumptions about the nature of people. Douglas McGregor identified two sets of assumptions: THEORY X involves assumptions that he feels supervisors often use as the basis for dealing with workers, while THEORY Y presents the assumptions that he feels supervisors should strive to use.

Theory X assumptions include:

- The average person has an inherent dislike for work and will avoid it if he/she can.
- Because of this characteristic, most people must be coerced, controlled, directed, and threatened with punishment to get them to put forth adequate effort to achieve goals.
- The average person prefers to be directed, wishes to avoid responsibility, has relatively little ambition, and wants security above all.

Theory Y assumptions include:

- The expenditure of physical and mental effort in work is as natural as play or rest.
- People will exercise self-direction and self-control in the service

of objectives to which they are committed.
- Commitment to objectives is a function of the rewards associated with achievement.

When McGregor introduced these ideas, he believed management practices were influenced primarily by Theory X assumptions. He felt managers were unnecessarily pessimistic in their view of people and that this pessimism led them to behave in ways that were too restrictive. He did not say that Theory X assumptions were always incorrect, but stressed that it was important to find the set of assumptions that best fit the employees being managed. McGregor said that there are times, many times, when Theory Y assumptions are a better fit than Theory X assumptions. His point was not that one or the other set was correct, although he was partial to Theory Y. His major point was that, whatever set of assumptions supervisors hold about people, those assumptions tend to affect our behavior as supervisors toward those people. Although it oversimplifies the complexity of human nature, this theory can have practical implications for supervisors if it serves as a stimulus for thinking about the assumptions that supervisors make about people at work.

Note that Ouchi and Reddin propose a *THEORY Z* which is an effectiveness dimension that implies that supervisors who use either Theory X **OR** Theory Z assumptions when dealing with people can be successful, depending on their **situation.**

Herzberg's Motivators and Hygiene Factors   EXHIBIT # 9

Frederick Herzberg's two-factor theory of motivation, also called the dual-factor theory and the motivator-hygiene theory, was based on his original study of 200 engineers and accountants. Herzberg concluded that two groups of factors influence workers' feelings about their jobs: motivators and hygienes (maintenance factors). The hygiene factors virtually have no effect on motivating workers and provide an almost neutral feeling among them. They are expected to exist and maintain, but do not necessarily improve, conditions. The second set of factors, the motivators or satisfiers, when present, cause job satisfaction and serve as motivators on the job. Absence of them will not necessarily cause dissatisfaction, but it will tend to reduce satisfaction. Herzberg believes that job satisfaction and job dissatisfaction should not be considered as opposite ends of the same continuum, but should be perceived as two separate and distinct dimensions. The opposite of "satisfaction" is "no satisfaction," and the opposite of "dissatisfaction" is "no dissatisfaction." Herzberg's motivators and hygiene factors follow.

HYGIENE *or MAINTENANCE Factors:*	*MOTIVATIONAL FACTORS* *or SATISFIERS:*
Company Policy and Administration	Opportunity for Achievement
Technical and Fair Supervision	Opportunity for Recognition
Relationship With Supervisor	Work Itself: Creative and Challenging
Relationship With Peers	
Relationship With Subordinates	Advancement
Salary	Personal Growth
Working Conditions	Responsibility
Job Security	Awards
Status	
Certain Benefits (medical/dental plans; vacation)	

Herzberg believed a worker who is "not dissatisfied" on the job is not necessarily motivated; he or she is simply in a relatively neutral state of no dissatisfaction. Only motivational factors can create satisfaction and they are on a separate scale. Therefore, managers who seek to eliminate factors that create job dissatisfaction can bring about peace, but not necessarily motivation. They will be placating their workers, rather than motivating them. When a hygiene factor such as salary is adequate, workers will not be dissatisfied, but neither will they be satisfied. He says increasing salary will not motivate workers to do a better job, but it will keep them from becoming dissatisfied. If managers want to motivate workers on their jobs, Herzberg suggests emphasizing achievement, recognition, a challenging job and his other motivators because they are intrinsically rewarding.

HYGIENES: When absent, increase dissatisfaction with the job. When present, prevent dissatisfaction but do not directly increase either satisfaction or motivation. Indirectly their presence is a necessary precondition for motivators to have their intended effect.

MOTIVATORS: When absent, prevent both satisfaction and motivation. When present, lead to satisfaction and motivation (IF hygienes are present).

Herzberg's theory has been criticized for his procedure, i.e. when things are going well, people tend to take credit themselves or contrarily, blame failure on the external environment. Also, some say the theory is an explanation of job satisfaction and is not a theory of motivation and assumes that a relationship between satisfaction and productivity exists. Regardless of criticisms, the theory has been widely read and has contributed to vertical expansion of jobs to allow workers greater responsibility.

The Vroom and Porter-Lawler Expectancy Models

The previously-presented theories all use needs as their core concept and they are often called content theories because they focus on WHAT needs motivate behavior. But focusing on needs is not the only way to examine motivation. Process theorists, like Vroom, Porter and Lawler, House, Adams, Locke, and Skinner focus on expectancy, equity, goal setting, and reinforcement processes and HOW individual behavior is energized, directed, maintained, and stopped.

The Vroom and Porter-Lawler Models are expectancy models which make two major assumptions about behavior: it is voluntary and it is directed toward achieving as much as possible of the things workers desire most. They argue that the strength of a tendency to act in a certain way depends on the strength of an expectation that the act will be followed by a given outcome and on the attractiveness of that outcome to the worker. It focuses on three motivational (M) relationships:

1) **EFFORT-PERFORMANCE.** The (mathematically calculated) probability perceived by the worker that exerting a given amount of effort will lead to performance (E or expectancy).

2) **PERFORMANCE-REWARD.** The degree (correlation coefficient) to which the worker believes that performing at a particular level will lead to attainment of a desired outcome (I or instrumentality).

3) **REWARDS-PERSONAL GOALS.** The degree to which organizational rewards satisfy a worker's personal goals or needs and the attractiveness of those potential rewards for the worker (V or valence).

In Expectancy Theory, the motivational equation is: $M = E \times I \times V$.

Expectancy Theory explains why a lot of workers are not motivated on their jobs and merely put forth the minimum effort necessary to get by. It suggests that workers' levels of effort (motivation) are not simply functions of rewards. Workers must feel that they have the ability to perform the task well (expectancy); they must feel that high performance is instrumental in receiving rewards; and they must value those rewards. If all three conditions are satisfied, workers will be motivated to exert greater effort. It recognizes that there is no universal principle for explaining everyone's motivations and that just because a manager understands what needs a worker seeks to satisfy does not ensure that the individual perceives high performance as necessarily leading to satisfaction of these needs. Expectancy Theory has the following **practical implications** for managers:

1) Determine what outcomes workers prefer and develop rewards that stimulate motivation.
2) Define, communicate, and clarify the specific level of performance that is desired to get the proper effort from workers.
3) Establish attainable performance goals to avoid frustration and confusion.

4) Link desired outcomes to performance goal achievement by defining how and when performance will be rewarded.

Porter and Lawler's Model stresses three other characteristics of the motivation process: the perceived value of a reward is determined by both intrinsic AND extrinsic rewards, the influence of an individual's perception of what is required to perform the task and the individual's ACTUAL ability to perform the task, and the perceived fairness of rewards influences the AMOUNT of satisfaction produced by those rewards.

EXHIBIT # 10

Hackman and Oldham's Job Characteristics Model

Hackman and Oldham's Job Characteristics Model (JCM) says that a job can be described in terms of five core job dimensions, as follows:

1) **SKILL VARIETY.** The degree to which the job requires a variety of different activities so the worker can use a number of different skills and abilities.
2) **TASK IDENTITY.** The degree to which the job requires completion of a whole and identifiable piece of work.
3) **TASK SIGNIFICANCE.** The degree to which the job has a substantial impact on the lives or work of other people.
4) **AUTONOMY.** The degree to which the job provides substantial freedom, independence, and discretion to the worker in scheduling the work and in determining the procedures to be used.
5) **FEEDBACK.** The degree to which carrying out the work activities required by the job results in the individual obtaining direct and clear information about the effectiveness of his or her performance.

The model says that if the first three dimensions exist in a job, the worker will view the job as important, valuable, and worthwhile. If jobs possess autonomy, workers will feel more personal responsibility for the results and that if a job provides feedback, the worker will know how effectively he or she is performing. The model presents three critical *psychological states* for workers: (1) experienced meaningfulness of the work, (2) experienced responsibility for outcomes of the work, and (3) knowledge of the actual results of the work. The model concludes that internal rewards are obtained by a worker when he or she LEARNS (knowledge of results) that he/she PERSONALLY (experienced responsibility) has performed well on a task he/she CARES about (experienced meaningfulness). The more these three states are present, the greater will be the worker's motivation, performance, and satisfaction. The links between the five job dimensions and four personal and work outcomes are moderated or adjusted by the strength of the individual's growth need for self-esteem and self-actualization. The four outcomes are: high internal work motivation, high-quality work performance, high satisfaction with the work, and low absenteeism and turnover.

Assessing A Job's Motivating Potential

The five core dimensions of the JCM can be combined into a single predictive index called the *Motivating Potential Score* (MPS), which suggests the motivation potential in a particular job. The MPS is calculated as follows for a job:

$$\text{MPS} = \frac{[\text{Skill Variety} + \text{Task Identity} + \text{Task Significance}]}{3} \times \text{Autonomy} \times \text{Feedback}$$

Jobs high on motivating potential must be high on at least one of the three factors that lead to experienced meaningfulness of work, and they must be high on both autonomy and feedback. If jobs score high on motivating potential, the model predicts that motivation, performance, and satisfaction will be positively affected, and the likelihood of absence and turnover will be lessened.

Useful Conclusions About Motivation

This section has emphasized the importance of managers understanding the "why" of human behavior in order to help them create a climate of positive motivation, so workers can motivate themselves. By understanding workers' needs, the complex motivation process, assumptions made by managers, several factors that influence performance, how workers behave in certain ways because of what they expect such behavior to achieve, how jobs should allow the worker autonomy, feedback, and control over work, and by understanding work design, managers can positively affect worker motivation for organizational and individual success.

Integrating The Motivational Concepts for Practical Implications

Blending Behavior, Values, Needs, and Motivation

There are a large number of motivation and needs theories and much complex information about behavior and values, but this section will blend and synthesize the many complex ideas into a set of useful guidelines for practical applications to help managers. The following are the most useful for building and maintaining a positive climate for motivation:

Positive Climate Guidelines

RECOGNIZE INDIVIDUAL DIFFERENCES. Because workers have many different needs, respect then and do not treat all individuals alike. Take the time initially in a relationship to get to know the workers personally and what's important to them, so you can individualize goals, level of participation, and rewards to match individual needs.

MATCH THE WORKER AND THE JOB. To the extent possible, match personal strengths and personalities with the demands of the task, so the people will be motivated to perform at a high level.

SPECIFY GOALS AND GIVE FEEDBACK. Ensure workers understand what they are supposed to be doing and give them regular information about how to get the job done and how they are progressing. Jointly develop specific goals and frequently provide feedback, especially deserved positive feedback which serves as an incentive for reinforcement and repeat performances.

ALLOW WORKER PARTICIPATION. Permit worker involvement in most, not all, decisions which affect them, e.g. setting work goals, choosing benefit packages, solving productivity and quality problems. This can increase productivity, commitment to goals, motivation, and job satisfaction.

PATIENTLY TELL WORKERS MISTAKES. When workers make mistakes, patiently tell them as soon as possible what they did wrong to ensure it will be done right the next time. Use this as a positive communication opportunity to convey the reason for the rule, rather than as punishment.

LINK REWARDS TO PERFORMANCE. Rewards must be contingent on performance and workers will work harder if they are sure of the rewards they can attain. Clearly link and deliver the rewards associated with performance criteria, so workers will not perceive a low relationship and exert low performance. Throughout the organization and for personnel decisions, differences in experience, skills, abilities, and efforts should actually explain differences in performance, pay, and other rewards.

NEVER MAKE PROMISES THAT CANNOT BE KEPT. Managers establish credibility and trust by keeping promises. Future resistance to change and decisions will be less, since personnel will trust the manager and put forth efforts because they will feel more secure.

REMOVE ROADBLOCKS. Effective managers understand that their workers will occasionally have trouble getting things done because of organizational roadblocks. Be flexible to assist workers when an order results in too much detail or redtape. Also, when sufficient resources are not available, fight to help the department and worker.

SERVE AS A ROLE MODEL. Follow organizational policies, procedures, and rules and set an example for workers, e.g. arrive to work on time, follow safety rules, be disciplined, show professional behavior.

Predicting Performance

Motivation is an individual's inner state that causes him or her to behave in a way that ensures the accomplishment of organizational goals. The more managers understand workers' behavior, the better they should be able to predict worker performance in various situations and influence it, so organizational goals can be achieved. Since productivity and effectiveness in ALL organizations are a result of the behavior of workers, anticipating and influencing this behavior and creating a positive climate for worker motivation and job satisfaction are of paramount importance. Most human behavior is rational and relatively predictable, so managers should seek to understand the "why" of it, recognizing that there are some variables uncontrollable to the worker and to the manager.

THE LEADERSHIP PROCESS

The Nature of Leadership

Leadership Issues

The leadership literature is voluminous and much of it is contradictory about its proper definition, its relationship to management, and the optimal approach to explaining it. It is a function of the personal characteristics and relationships of the leader and follower(s), the complexity of the task, and of the elements of the specific situation. In general, there are trait models, leader behavior models, and situational or contingency models for leadership. While there are hundreds of definitions of "leadership," the author simply defines it as:

THE PROCESS OF INFLUENCING OTHERS TO WORK WILLINGLY TOWARD ACHIEVING SHARED GOALS AND OBJECTIVES.

Cultural Variables

Important variables often overlooked in the determination of leadership effectiveness are *national and organizational cultures.* The national culture affects leadership style by shaping preferences of leaders and defining what is acceptable to subordinates. In essence, **leaders cannot choose their styles at will** because they are constrained by the cultural conditions of their country in which they have been socialized and which has influenced what their followers have come to expect. An organization's culture shapes a leader's behavior by influencing the selection of leaders and the values that effective leaders are expected to demonstrate.

Characteristics of Effective Followers

With so much attention centered around the leader's traits and behaviors and the organization's culture and situational variables, the followers are often overlooked. Most certainly, followers are of critical importance in accomplishing results. Followers differ in the qualities they bring to the leadership process and their behaviors must be adjusted and guided by leaders to accomplish desired organizational goals. Studies reported in the Harvard Business Review by R. E. Kelley indicate that the following follower qualities are common in effective followers:

- They manage themselves well and are able to think for themselves, work independently, and without close supervision.

- They are committed to a purpose outside of themselves, like an idea, a work team, a product, an organization, a cause, etc.

- They build their competence and focus their efforts for maximum impact; they hold higher performance standards than their job or work group requires; they master special skills of use to their organization.

- They are courageous, honest, and credible; they establish themselves as independent, critical thinkers, whose knowledge and judgment can be trusted; they hold high ethical standards.

Power

A key component of effective leadership is the legitimate position *power* the leader has to affect other people's behavior and get them to act in certain ways. Certainly, excessive use of coercive power seldom produces high performance and is questionable ethically. The giving or withholding of tangible (e.g. pay, job assignment) and intangible (e.g. praise, respect) rewards should not be used like a "carrot-and-stick", but rather as a signal that workers are doing a fine job and that their efforts are appreciated.

The Trait Model

These early models of leadership sought to determine what effective leaders are like as people and what they do that makes them effective. Researchers like Ralph Stogdill thought that effective leaders must have certain common personal qualities that set them apart from ineffective leaders and reported this in the Journal of Psychology in 1948. Trait researchers described traits of individuals in leadership positions by such characteristics as charismatic, enthusiastic, courageous, intelligent, self-confident, dominant, and honest. They thought leaders who do not possess these traits or inherited characteristics could be ineffective. It has come to be recognized that traits alone are not the key to understanding leader effectiveness. Some effective leaders do not possess all of these traits, and some who do are not effective in their leadership roles. *There is NOT a consistent relationship between leader traits and leader effectiveness.* Generally, leaders are made, not born.

Leader Behavior Models

The failure to identify predictive leadership traits led researchers to turn to looking at what good leaders do, their behavior. There are four key leader behavior models which will be generally explored: Blake and Mouton's Managerial Grid, Tannenbaum and Schmidt's Continuum, the Ohio State University Studies, and the University of Michigan Studies.

Blake and Mouton's Managerial Grid

One model that looks at the behavior of the leader and his or her style along two dimensions is Blake and Mouton's Managerial Grid. Its two dimensions are the concern for *PEOPLE* and the concern for *PRODUCTION*, depicted on separate axes. The grid has nine positions along each axis, creating 81 different positions for a leader's style. Proponents focus on the extreme styles 1,1; 1,9; 9,1; and 9,9 and claim that effective leaders use a 9,9 style, the highest concern for production and for people. Researchers today believe that there are more dimensions than just the two considered in this early model.

Tannenbaum and Schmidt's Continuum

This model is a range or continuum of leadership behavior available to managers when they are making decisions. Tannenbaum and Schmidt define seven types of leadership behavior which emphasize decision making and the use of authority by the manager and the amount of freedom allowed for subordinates. The following are the seven types of leadership behavior in this model:

1). **The manager makes the decision and announces it.** The manager identifies the problem, chooses the solution, and requires followers to implement the chosen alternative (*tells*).

2). **The manager "*sells*" the decision.** As above, the manager identifies and solves the problem, but rather than announcing it for implementation, he or she tries to persuade subordinates to accept it.

3). **The manager presents ideas and invites questions.** This is like the previous type, with the addition of subordinates being invited to ask questions.

4). **The manager presents a tentative decision that is subject to change.** The manager allows workers to have some part in the decision making process, but retains the responsibility for identifying and diagnosing the problem. The final decision is made by the manager.

5). **The manager presents the problem, gets suggestions, and then makes the decision.** This approach allows the subordinates the opportunity to offer problem solutions before the manager does. The manager, however, identifies the problem (*consults*).

6). **The manager defines the limits and asks the group to make a decision.** The manager defines the problem and sets boundaries, but then enters into a partnership with workers to arrive at a decision.

7). **The manager permits the group to make decisions within prescribed limits.** The manager becomes an equal member of the group and the group identifies the problem, develops possible solutions, and chooses a solution (*joins*).

Ohio State University Studies

The Ohio State University (OSU) studies concluded that leaders exhibit two main types of behavior:

- **Initiating Structure Behavior.** Delineates the relationship between the leader and followers; establishes well-defined patterns of organization, communication, and procedures to follow in the performance of tasks.

- **Consideration Behavior.** Reflects friendship, mutual trust, respect, support, and warmth in the relationship between leader and followers; caring and human relations behavior

A Leader Behavior Description Questionnaire (LBDQ) was developed at OSU for measuring the two dimensions. After analysis of the leader behaviors, the result was a model that depicts four fundamental leadership styles, each being a different combination of leader consideration and structure behaviors:

- Low Structure, High Consideration
- Low Structure, Low Consideration
- High Structure, High Consideration
- High Structure, Low Consideration

The OSU researchers found in general that the study group's productivity was NOT affected in a usual way by leadership style. For instance, the most proficient production departments tended to have structuring leaders, but the most proficient non-production units tended to be managed by considerate leaders. However, there were exceptions and inconsistencies. In general, the research results are inconsistent and inconclusive. It seems that in most situations, considerate leaders would have more satisfied subordinates and that structured leaders would have more grievances filed, but we must be careful in making these conclusions and must note that <u>what is a successful leadership style in one situation may prove ineffective in another situation.</u>

University of Michigan Studies

Rensis Likert and his associates at the University of Michigan identified two leadership styles. **Employee-oriented leaders** who focus on the individuality and personality needs of employees and emphasize building good interpersonal relationships. **Job-oriented leaders** who focus on production, the job's technical aspects, and the work a subordinate is doing. The results of the OSU and Michigan studies are very similar. Both indicated two primary dimensions of leader behavior, a work dimension and a people dimension and both had inconsistencies. Likert, however, concluded in his 1961 book New Patterns of Management that supervisors with the best record of performance focus their primary attention on the human aspects of their subordinates' problems and on endeavoring to build effective work groups with high performance goals. Other Michigan researchers, Day and Hamblin, found in subsequent studies in 1964 that no consistent relationship emerged between closeness of supervision and employee performance.

Situational Models

Leadership situations are so varied that deciding to use one style as the most effective one is an *oversimplification*, so situational models have arisen which link a style with an appropriate situation. This may also be an oversimplification, because there are many situational variables which operate in many different situations. Different styles may prove effective (or ineffective) in a single situation, if only one of the many factors vary slightly in a certain direction. It seems as if almost every time one tries to make a definitive conclusion on an appropriate leadership style or issue, there must be qualification to reflect one or more situational factors. Thus, the situational or contingency models of leadership have arisen.

Fiedler's Contingency Model

The first comprehensive attempt to develop a situational approach to leadership was presented by Fred Fiedler working at the University of Illinois in the mid-1960s. He proposed that effective group performance depends on the proper match between the leader's style and the degree to which the situation or context gives control and influence to the leader. Fiedler believed that leadership style is an enduring characteristic, that managers cannot generally change their style, nor adopt different styles in different kinds of situations. So, he identified *three situational characteristics or variables* that are important determinants of how favorable a situation is for leading:

1). **Leader-member relations.** The degree of confidence, trust, and respect subordinates have in their leader, either good or bad.
2) **Task structure.** The degree to which the subordinate's job assignments are structured, either high or low.
3). **Position power.** The degree of influence a leader has over variables such as hiring, firing, discipline, promotions, and salary increases, either strong or weak.

When a situation is favorable for leading, it is relatively easy for a manager to influence subordinates so that they perform at a high level and contribute to organizational effectiveness. In a situation unfavorable for leading, it is much more difficult for a manager to exert influence. By taking all possible combinations of good and bad leader-member relations, high and low task structure, and strong and weak position power, *Fiedler identified eight leadership situations*, which vary in their favorability for leading.

Fiedler determined that relationship-oriented leaders are most effective in moderately favorable situations (e.g. weak position power, low task structure, and good leader-member relations) and task-oriented leaders are most effective in very favorable (e.g. strong position power, high task structure, good leader-member relations) or very unfavorable situations (weak position power, low task structure, bad leader-member relations). EXHIBIT # 11 shows the 8 possible styles.

EXHIBIT 11

FIEDLER'S CONTINGENCY LEADERSHIP MODEL

Leader-Member Relations	Good 1	Good 2	Good 3	Good 4	Poor 1	Poor 2	Poor 3	Poor 4
Task Structure	High	High	Weak	Weak	High	High	Weak	Weak
Position Power	Strong	Weak	Strong	Weak	Strong	Weak	Strong	Weak
Leadership STYLE	C☆ A S	C A S	C A S	P✸ P C	P P C	P P C	M◯ 	M

☆ CAS: Controlling; Active; Structured Leadership Style

✸ PPC: Permissive; Passive; Considerate Leadership Style

◯ M: Middle-Ground (Between CAS and PPC) Leadership

A practical application of Fiedler's model suggests for effectiveness that managers need to be placed in leadership situations that fit their style or situations need to be changed to suit the manager. Remember that he believes that a leader's style is an enduring characteristic that managers cannot change. Situations, however, can be changed by giving a manager more position power or taking steps to increase task structure, such as by clarifying goals.

House's Path-Goal Model

Robert House focused on what leaders can do to motivate their subordinates to achieve group and organizational goals. The premise of his Path-Goal Model is that effective leaders motivate subordinates to achieve goals by (1) clearly identifying the outcomes that subordinates are trying to obtain from the workplace, (2) rewarding subordinates with these outcomes for high performance and the attainment of work goals, and (3) clarifying for subordinates the *paths* leading to the attainment of work *goals.* It is a contingency model because it proposes that the steps that managers should take to motivate subordinates depend on both the nature of the subordinates and the type of work they do.

Based on the expectancy theory of motivation (see Vroom and Porter-Lawler Expectancy Models of Motivation), path-goal theory provides managers with three guidelines for effective leadership:

1) **Learn what outcomes your subordinates want to obtain from their jobs and the organization.** After identifying them (pay, work hours, assignments), the manager should make sure that he/she has the reward power needed to distribute or withhold them.

2) **Reward subordinates for high performance and goal attainment with the outcomes they desire.** For example, distribute pay raises or give job assignments to those earning them to the extent that they performed highly on the identified dimensions.

3) **Clarify the paths to goal attainment for subordinates, remove obstacles to high performance, and express confidence in subordinates' capabilities.** This does not mean that managers need to TELL his or her subordinates what to do. Rather, that a manager needs to make sure that subordinates are clear about what they should be trying to accomplish and have the capabilities, resources, and confidence needed to be successful.

Path-goal theory identifies four kinds of behaviors that leaders can engage in to motivate subordinates:

★   **Directive Behaviors.** Setting goals, showing workers how to complete tasks, taking solid steps to improve performance.

★   **Supportive Behaviors.** Expressing concern for workers and looking out for their best interests.

★   **Participative Behaviors.** Giving workers a voice in matters and decisions that affect them.

★   **Achievement-Oriented Behaviors.** Setting very challenging goals, expecting that they be met, and believing in their capabilities.

This model concludes that the behaviors that managers should use to lead effectively depends, or is contingent, on the nature of the subordinates and the kind of work they do. For example, leader directive behaviors may be beneficial when subordinates are having difficulty completing assigned tasks, but could be detrimental when they are independent thinkers who work best when left alone. Likewise, achievement-oriented behaviors may increase motivation for highly-capable subordinates who are bored from having too few challenges, but may not work if used with subordinates who are already pushed to their limit.

<u>**Effective managers must know their own and followers' behaviors, define the dimensions of the various situations they find themselves in, and determine what kinds of leader behaviors work best for them for success in the different situations.**</u>

Hersey-Blanchard's Life Cycle Model

The situational leadership model or the Hersey-Blanchard Life Cycle Model (HBLC) uses the same two dimensions that Fiedler identified: task behavior (horizontal axis) and relationship behavior (vertical axis). However, they go a step farther by considering each as either high or low and then combine them into four specific leader behaviors:

- **Telling.** High task, low relationship; leader defines roles and tells workers what, how, when, and where to do tasks; directive

- **Selling.** High task, high relationship; leader provides both directive and supportive behaviors.

- **Participating.** Low task, high relationship; leader and follower share in decision making; leader is primarily facilitator

- **Delegating.** Low task, low relationship; leader provides little direction or support

Another dimension of the HBLC Model is the *"maturity"* or follower readiness variable. Maturity is the subordinates ability to perform their job independently, to assume additional responsibility, their desire to achieve success, and their willingness to effectively deal with the task environment. They define four stages of maturity for followers:

R1. Followers are both unable and unwilling to take responsibility to do something.

R2. Followers are unable, but willing to do job tasks; motivated but currently lack skills.

R3. Followers are able, but unwilling to do what leader wants.

R4. Followers are both able and willing to do what is asked of them.

The HBLC Model proposes a curvilinear relationship among the leader's task behavior, relationship behavior, and the maturity of the followers. Leadership style should reflect the maturity level of followers. As the level of maturity of the followers increases, appropriate leader behavior requires less of both structuring and socio-emotional support from the leader. It suggests that leader behavior should move from (1) high task- low relationship behavior to (2) high task- high relationship behavior, and from (3) high relationship- low task behavior to (4) low task- low relationship behavior, as one's subordinates progress from immaturity to maturity. A manager's leadership style will be effective only if it is appropriate for the maturity level of the followers. Managers should recognize that there is limited scientific investigation verifying this theory, so it should be applied very carefully. Researchers have identified so many situational factors that have at least some bearing on the leader's effectiveness that this results in confusion and inconclusiveness about recommendations as to how leaders can improve. However, a leader's style, the followers' characteristics, and the situational variables do significantly interact and considerably effect an organization's success. See EXHIBIT # 12.

EXHIBIT 12

HERSEY-BLANCHARD LIFE CYCLE LEADERSHIP MODEL

EFFECTIVE LEADER BEHAVIOR

RELATIONSHIP BEHAVIOR

HIGH RELATIONSHIP AND LOW TASK S3	HIGH TASK AND HIGH RELATIONSHIP S2
LOW RELATIONSHIP AND LOW TASK S4	HIGH TASK AND LOW RELATIONSHIP S1

TASK BEHAVIOR

MATURE ← FOLLOWER → IMMATURE

LEADERSHIP STYLES:

S1 = TELLING

S2 = SELLING

S3 = PARTICIPATING

S4 = DELEGATING

Transformational Leadership

Concept and Definition

A new form of leadership emerged in the 1980s called **transformational leadership**. Influenced by James Burns' 1978 book called Leadership which argued that leadership could be viewed as either a transactional or a transformational process. He suggested that leader behaviors are based on *quid pro quo* transactions which are more focused on accomplishing the tasks at hand, by adapting the leader's style and behavior to accommodate the follower's expectations. He said it is often not a transactional, but a TRANSFORMATIONAL style of leadership that is required to manage change. Transactional and transformational leadership should not be viewed as opposing approaches to getting things done. Transformational leadership should be built on top of the necessary ground level of transactional leadership.

Seltzer and Bass in their 1990 article in the Journal of Management say that transformational leadership refers to the process of influencing major changes in the attitudes and assumptions of organization members and building commitment for the organization's mission, objectives, and strategies. In essence, these transformational leaders bring about change, innovation, a vision, entrepreneurship, and revitalization.

Characteristics of Transformational Leaders

EXHIBIT # 13

TRANSFORMATIONAL LEADERS:

❑
Are *charismatic* by providing a vision and sense of mission, instilling pride, and gaining respect and trust.

- Are *inspirational* in that the leader passionately communicates a future idealistic organization that can be shared.

- Go beyond being *considerate* and treat employees as individuals and stress development and self-actualization.

- Use *intellectual stimulation* to encourage employees to discover creative methods of confronting problems.

Productivity and Satisfaction Relationship

It seems clear that a transformational style of leadership can be very effective, especially for a situation that requires managing dramatic change. Bass and Avolio conclude in their 1992 article in the Journal of European Industrial Training that transformational leadership is more strongly correlated with lower turnover rates, higher productivity, and higher employee satisfaction.

Leadership Conclusions

The understanding of leadership is complex with many dimensions, behaviors, and variables involved in diverse situations. The following are some general conclusions about leadership:

1. Leadership is complex and problematic. Often, leadership effectiveness is defined emotionally and subjectively in terms of perception and feelings, which may not align with any objective measure of effectiveness.

2. Certain traits do seem to be related to the perception of leadership, but possessing these traits is no guarantee of success. The leader characteristics that one organizational culture values are not necessarily transferrable to another organization.

3. Previous experiences in a leadership position and past successes or failures are not of significant use in predicting leadership effectiveness, because of differences and incompatibility in *situations*.

4. Regardless of actual effectiveness, people subjectively characterize individuals as "leaders" when they have traits such as intelligence, outgoing personality, strong verbal skills, aggressiveness, understanding, and when they exhibit high-people and high-task behaviors.

5. Leader effectiveness is enhanced by having followers who exhibit effective follower behaviors and have a high level of maturity.

6. The actions and behaviors of a leader are influenced by a follower's personality, experience, ability, and motivation.

7. Participation, involvement of employees, and giving employees the freedom to use their abilities as they think best must be recognized by successful leaders in contemporary organizations in certain situations, with less emphasis on controlling people and work tasks.

8. The proper amount of employee participation in decision making has been found to be heavily influenced by situational factors, such as quality requirements, subordinate commitment, and conflicts over options.

9. There is NO leadership style that is consistently effective.

10. Key situational or contingency factors determining leadership effectiveness include task structure, goals and objectives, leader position power, leader-member relations, follower characteristics and maturity, organizational culture, the work group, and national culture.

CONTROLLING AND MANAGING TIME

Basic Planning and Time Management

Time is the scarcest organizational, and personal, resource and no one can create more time nor bring back time that has passed. Time is a unique resource, since everyone has the same amount. So, managers must manage the available time to meet deadlines and get work done. Given that unforeseen problems arise, that usually most activities consume more time than expected, and that managers do not have control over all of their time, managers must be proactive and answer the questions: Where does my time go? Where should my time go? How can I use my time better? Basic planning and organization techniques can utilize time optimally and save time.

Inventory of Personal Time Utilization

To answer the question of "Where does my time go?", managers must develop a time log to gather reliable data and analyze past time activities. This will enable managers to learn some of their less desirable work habits and patterns and help decide which activities and behaviors should be eliminated, modified, or delegated to others. One method for analyzing managerial activities is to keep a daily activities log for at least two weeks and then transfer the information to a weekly activities log. While this log activity appears to be a time user itself, the benefits can far exceed the additional time cost. Pick a typical work week and keep track of all your time and what you are doing with it. Record your time use at least every half hour and make comments about special inefficiencies or problems, e.g. if a task took longer than expected, if you were interpreted, or if there was a wait delay. After you keep a daily log for two weeks, summarize the information in a weekly log so you can see patterns. You will discover that you use your time differently than you think.

Time Use Quiz

EXHIBIT # 14

In addition to gathering actual data from daily and weekly time logs, take the following quiz and review the answers to gather more data to help you with your time management.

Answer the ten questions below about various ways of approaching a job based on your characteristic work habit patterns. Make one checkmark in a column for each item.

TIME USE QUIZ

	ALMOST ALWAYS	SOMETIMES	OFTEN	ALMOST NEVER
1. I keep a written log of how I spend my major portions of my working day.				
2. I schedule my least desirable tasks at a time when my energy is at its peak.				
3. I find the opportunity to let someone else do a job that I can do better.				
4. I have time to do what I want to do and what I should do in performing my job.				
5. I examine my job to determine how I can combine or eliminate activities.				
6. Actions that lead to short-run objectives take preference over those that might be more important in the long run.				

7. My supervisor assigns more work than he/she thinks I can handle.

8. I attack short-time tasks (answering phone calls, reading correspondence, etc.) before projects taking a long time.

9. I review the sequence of my job activities and make necessary improvements.

10. I arrange task priorities based on the importance of task goals.

TIME USE QUIZ OPTIMAL ANSWERS

1. SOMETIMES. While keeping a log can help eliminate useless effort, it can be a time waster if you are preoccupied with maintaining it, so be time conscious with an occasional informal review but do not keep a continuous daily record.

2. ALMOST ALWAYS. Schedule the least interesting, most difficult, and least desirable tasks when your energy is at its greatest, usually first thing in the MORNING. Do not do the pleasurable and enjoyable tasks first; put off those things you do well until the END of the day when energy is usually lowest, after the difficult, complex, and least interesting tasks. Generally, most productive time is 9 to 11 a.m. and 2 to 4 p.m., with the morning being more productive than the afternoon.

3. ALMOST ALWAYS. The effective manager should not be concerned with doing ALL jobs perfectly, but in trading off quality with cost. There is an optimal quality level and there is a diminishing returns level of effort. Many are victimized by their inquisitive drive for excellence in EVERY task and feel that they must always do the highest quality work possible and maintain very close tolerances, even though this

is not ALWAYS required and is very expensive to maintain. The supervisor who insists on doing all key work himself because he is the only one who can do it to perfection, is wasting his time and needlessly increasing the cost to the organization (suboptimization).

4. ALMOST ALWAYS. Time should be available as needed, according to priorities and according to the total development concept: mental, physical, spiritual, and social growth. Time should be planned for appropriate activities in these areas according to goals and priorities for LONG-TERM effectiveness.

5. SOMETIMES. Real time consciousness will dictate this activity be performed occasionally, but it is NOT necessary for formal analysis on a constant basis. Follow suggested time management guidelines.

6. SOMETIMES. The optimal situation is to attain short-run AND long-run objectives concurrently. The long-run objective may NOT always be the most important one, since your supervisor dictates priorities. Do not get in a trade-off position. Sometimes if the short-run is not attended to, the long-run will not exist. However, long-run goals must be served and SOMETIMES at the short-run expense.

7. ALMOST NEVER. Work loads should be assigned based on skills, abilities, available resources, and priority goals, rather than personality quirks. If the supervisor believes a worker is wasting time doing unnecessary tasks, this time management quality problem should be dealt with, rather than increase the quantity of tasks. If more resources are required, this management problem should be addressed.

8. ALMOST NEVER. It is possible to spend the entire day handling short-time-required, routine details and urgent tasks, while getting prepared for the more important tasks. Address important tasks before routine and frequent ones by blocking time for large projects, starting large jobs at the start of the day and pursuing them to completion, etc. Use phone answering system and/or secretary to screen.

9. OFTEN. Proper sequencing of the order, time use, and sometimes cost

of job activities is very important for long-run success. Without frequent review, even informal ones, the timing of long-run projects may be affected. Several project control techniques exist, e.g. PERT, CPM, flow diagrams.

10. ALMOST ALWAYS. Know your goals for all projects and activities and then prioritize your tasks and efforts accordingly. Your goals and objectives must be specified first. Importance comes before urgency. The amount of time spent on each of your efforts MUST be directly and proportionately related to the priorities of your goals and activities.

Time Management Concepts

ABC Analysis is a concept to assist you with the prediction that 80 percent of your time will be spent on only 20 percent of your problems, called the *80/20 Rule*. To work with this problem situation, the 20 percent of the problems that you work on should be rated as class A, the very important and vital ones. Class B items are not quite so important as A items. Class C problems are ranked the lowest in importance, even though there are many of them. Plan to concentrate your time beginning with the A items, the few very important ones, then the B items, and let the trivial many C ones wait their turn. The challenge is how do you recognize the vital few A items. Usually they are recognizable because your supervisor has pinpointed them for you and experience will help. You may waste a few hours the first time on what turns out to be an inconsequential problem. The next time it surfaces you will know how to dispose of it quickly or that you should put it down on your priority list.

Importance and Time Allocation

To help judge a problem's **importance** and your **time allocation**, ask yourself these questions:

1. Where did it come from? The source usually dictates the priority and amount of delay time available. Of course, a directive from your manager

or your manager's manager is of top importance.

2. What is its potential for trouble? Remember minor problems can have great potential for trouble. Consider if the unresolved problem directly affects results, goals, production, and productivity. Is it in the main sequence of activities or related to outside or external relationships or goals.

3. Is it aimed at results rather than activity? Rather than spend so much time on routine and repetitive (but necessary) activities, focus time efforts on getting results in terms of goals and greater quality, output, or lower costs.

4. How quickly can it be disposed of? Be careful of this situation, since many problems on the surface look as if they can be quickly handled. The temptation is to immediately plunge into them without initially carefully thinking. These problems can easily turn into major time consumption and many headaches. Take the time initially to think through the aspects of the problem and what might happen, to save time in the long run. Tasks that can be handled quickly should be grouped together and finished in one block of time, usually at the end of the day. Problems requiring major efforts should be planned when your energy is at its peak, usually in the morning, and when you can block sufficient time.

5. Can it be delegated? If someone else can do the urgent task for you and solve the problem while meeting the minimal required standards, then probably it is not important enough to be at the very top of your priority list, relative to your major problems. Do not get caught giving your priorities to many trivial jobs, while putting your challenging problem on hold. Take on the big job first and delegate the urgent and routine jobs.

Time Management Philosophy

Facts, Assumptions, and Attitude

No matter what our position is, what our title is, how much money we earn, what our responsibilities are, nor what our goals and objectives are, we all have 86,400 seconds in each day and 604,800 seconds in a week... the same amount of time. For all of us time passed is history and time to come is an assumption. The time is now in the present, so we have to use it wisely to accomplish what is important to us, personally and professionally, our goals and objectives.

TIME USE MUST BE DIRECTLY RELATED TO WHAT IS IMPORTANT TO US.

Because time is related to effectiveness and output, we must develop personal time control habits and allocate out time directly to important results desired. Time balance and time management in all areas of our life are necessary for total life effectiveness.

Managers work a full day, have a hectic pace, and are constantly on the go with many problems and situations to handle. Just as managers have job responsibilities listed and duties to manage, the manager should accept the responsibility to regularly manage his or her time, to get the organizational results. Having the right **attitude** toward time management is a big first step. Your daily attitude must be to get as much important work done as possible, in the shortest possible time. Your attitude should accept the approach that you start every day with a major project that is important to results, with other lesser important projects and routine, trivial activities to follow later. Make projects that are directly related to organizational priorities your top priorities in effort given and time utilized.

Self-Management System

Know Goals, Objectives, and Priorities:

By knowing your *PERSONAL* goals, objectives, and priorities, you can better manage yourself and better manage your *JOB* responsibilities, goals, objectives, priorities. You can optimally accomplish personal and organizational results because your effectiveness habits are intertwined and follow naturally.

While you are in control of your time and activities, tools are available to assist you. You should control and manage the tool, not let it control you. In addition to the desktop computer scheduling systems and e-mail programs, there are several proven tools that can help the supervisor add more value to your time by improving the ways that you plan and organize your activities.

Useful Time Management Tools:

The following tools are suggested for your use:

POCKET-SIZED APPOINTMENT BOOKS. This is a readily-available portable reference to, and record of, appointments and planned activities, when you are away from your desk, office, or organization. Be sure and keep it coordinated with your desk calendar, computer, and secretary. *THIS IS A MUST!*

DAILY PLANNER. This tool lists all planned daily activities and the specific times that you intend to perform them, so you can see the whole daily picture at a glance. Your office desk calendar or your computer calendar can double as a daily planner as well. A weekly planner may be used to see a week at a glance.

ELECTRONIC PLANNER. Various small, personalized electronic computerized diaries and planners are available to assist with time management, but recognize that batteries may be required and information can be lost.

ABC LISTS. Preprinted lists of things to do with priority columns are available or can be constructed by individuals for use as a tool. Supervisors can give these to workers to assist them.

The point is to have a personal self-management system for time control that you are comfortable with, whatever that may be.

Guidelines for Time Success

The following are *TOP 10 TIME MANAGEMENT GUIDELINES* offered to assist you with organizing your work and managing your time:

1. Take the time up front to plan and organize your work, establishing realistic goals and priorities.

2. Establish A-B-C priorities for using your time based on *importance*, not urgency.

3. Make a daily "To-Do" List of work you need to do, at the end of every day.

4. Perform the most difficult tasks when you have a high energy level, usually in the mornings.

5. Return letters and memos with responses as notes in the margins.

6. Use a note pad to jot down key ideas that come to mind and for follow-up.

7. Group ROUTINE tasks for accomplishment at certain times of the day, such as telephone calls or recordkeeping, and set aside a specific time for them, e.g. between 8:00 and 9:00 a.m. and between 4:00 and 5:00 p.m. each day.

8. Delegate appropriate work according to abilities and demands of workers to ensure effectiveness. Do not *suboptimize* by attempting to do everything yourself.

9. Act decisively and do not procrastinate for important decisions; handle paper only once.

10. Tactfully say "no" to excessive time demands, relative to established goals and priorities.

Time Management Problems and Suggestions

Specific Problems and Solutions

Some common time wasters and suggested solutions are offered for your consideration:

1. **Telephone Interruptions:**   Unnecessary Calls

       Possible Causes: Lack of self discipline
   Desire to be informed & involved

       Solutions: Screen & group calls; be brief; stay uninvolved with all but essentials; manage by exception; conference calls; use e-mail

2. **Visitors Without Appointments:**

       Possible Causes: Enjoyment of socializing; inability to say "no" or to state priorities

       Solutions: Meet visitors outside; suggest lunch if necessary; hold stand-up conferences; say "no"; be unavailable; modify open-door policy; do it elsewhere; screen

3. **Lack of Planning:**

   Possible Causes: Failure to see the benefit; action oriented; success without it

   Solutions: Emphasize results... not activity; recognize that planning takes time, but saves time in the end; recognize that success is often in spite of, not because of, methods

4. **Lack of Priorities and Deadlines:**

   Possible Causes: Lack of goals and objectives; not systems oriented; bogged down in daily routine; not results oriented

   Solutions: Written goals & objectives; discuss priorities with subordinates & team; respond first to important, not urgent; distinguish between short and long run tasks; concentrate first and most on most important & what is more directly related to objectives; see if tasks can be combined or delegated; give more value to total organization than your department

5. **Over commitment/Too Much At Once:**

   Possible Causes: Broad interests; confusion in priorities; failure to set priorities; achievement and personal desires detract from total organization goals

   Solutions: Say "no"; put first things first within the firm and outside the firm and then totally; develop a philosophy of time; relate priorities to a schedule of events

6. **Crisis Management/Fire Fighting:**

   Possible Causes: Lack of planning; unrealistic time estimates; problem orientation (solely); reluctance of subordinates to break bad news; activity orientation; not distinguishing between important & urgent tasks

   Solutions: Apply same solutions as for lack of planning; allow for interruptions in time planning; be primarily opportunity/goal oriented, rather than process-oriented; encourage fast transmission of information as essential for timely corrective action; distinguish between important & urgent and the result and the activity; don't hesitate to use the back burner or "hold" mode

7. Scheduled and Unscheduled Meetings:

Possible Causes: Fear of responsibility for decisions; indecision; over communication; poor leadership

Solutions: Make decisions even when some facts are missing; be willing to take calculated risks; make decisions without meetings; discourage unnecessary meetings; convene only those needed; use agendas; stick to the subject; have brief meetings; prepare concise minutes ASAP; set time limits & stick to them

8. Cluttered Desk/ Stacked Desk:

Possible Causes: Personal disorganization; covering up inefficiency; an excuse for poor productivity; desire to create busy image

Solutions: Plan a catch-up time for reorganizing; use the wastebasket hourly; have a desk system; put only priority items on your desk use daily accordion file; clear desk before leaving each day; put photos on side table

9. **Routine/Trivia/Unimportant Tasks:**

    Possible Causes: Allow impulses and spur-of-the-moment decisions to rule; lack of priorities; refusal to delegate; feeling of greater security with detail

    Solutions: Set & concentrate on goals & objectives; delegate nonessentials; look to results not details nor methods

10. **Hasty Style:**

    Possible Causes: Impatience with detail; responding to urgent not important; lack of planning; prefer technical rather than managerial work; attempting too much in too little time

    Solutions: Place important before urgent; attempt less; delegate more; take time to plan; take time to do it right to save time of doing it over; find a hideaway or have a quiet hour built into schedule

11. **Paperwork and Reading:**

Possible Causes:	Failure to screen; knowledge explosion; computeritis
Solutions:	80/20 rule; delegate reading to subordinates; have secretary screen material; read selectively; learn speed reading & shorthand; handle each paper only once; annotate memo/letter in pen rather than type; use phone or e-mail rather than write letters

12. **Indecision:**

Possible Causes:	Lack of confidence in facts/subordinates; omnipotent me attitude; insistence on all facts; fear of consequences of a mistake; lack decision making process
Solutions:	Accept risks as inevitable; decide without ALL facts; improve fact-finding & validating procedures; delegate the right to be occasionally wrong; use mistakes as learning process; follow scientific method; do unpleasant tasks first

Managing Interruptions

Unexpected arrivals of customers, supervisors, suppliers, and other workers are a normal part of the workplace. Drop-ins interrupt your schedule and conversations often digress beyond reasons for the visit. Your secretary, if you have one, can perform a valuable screening function, but you still have to use judgment in handling these visitors. You may encourage visits by your expressed desire to keep informed about everything and your enjoyment of socializing, but you have to be able to communicate your specific desires. You should always be available to be interrupted by your manager. There are several techniques for handling drop-in visitors. A partially closed door can indicate that you are busy. The straight forward approach is best, politely explaining that you do not have time to visit and another time would be best. Standing while you talk also indicates that your time is short. You can greet the visitor at the door or move outside to the hallway and be alert for an appropriate point to end the conversation. Scheduling working lunches away from your office present opportunities for concurrent work and lunch to conserve time and a chance to leave early from lunch at your convenience. Limiting idle social chatting to 3 or 4 minutes or so at the end of the day, recognizes the separation between social conversation and business-related discussions.

General Time Saving Techniques

Self-discipline, which requires persistence in efforts to reach objectives, is the key to success in any activity. It is a combination of attitude, desire, persistence, and confidence. A good self-discipline strategy to minimize wasted time is to do work in **blocks of time** of at least two hours a block and , when possible, away from your office in a private room or **"hideaway"**. This allows you to continuously concentrate your efforts without interruptions, so your mind does not wander or get distracted by telephone calls, drop-ins, or other routine projects or activities. **Meetings** are also a natural part of work life and they can be nonproductive timewasters. It is important to hold meetings only when necessary, since prescheduled meetings tend to fill the time set aside. Meetings can be prescheduled, as staff meetings every week, but if little important information is available for one week, the meeting can be canceled and the information presented at next week's meeting. A meeting just to have a general meeting is a timewaster for everyone. Controlling **paperwork flow** is another technique of saving time. Paperwork can be controlled as it crosses your desk by handling it only once, or at least a minimum number of times. Make and keep photocopies of only very important paperwork, or sparingly as needed. Making **notes in margins** of letters and memos will cut response time. Use the **wastebasket** rather than the file cabinet and throw out all unnecessary papers; use computer files as backups. Do not remain idle when **waiting**, use the time to read C priority memos or business articles or make a rough draft of a letter.

EXHIBIT # 15

A Work Priority System

Use the following priority system to manage your work time:

A PRIORITY SYSTEM FOR RELATING TO WORK ACTIVITIES

A. INTRINSIC IMPORTANCE

VERY IMPORTANT	IMPORTANT	NOT SO IMPORTANT	UNIMPORTANT
Must be done	Should be done	May not be necessary, but may be useful	Can be eliminated entirely
1	2	3	4

B. URGENCY

VERY URGENT	URGENT	NOT URGENT	TIME IS NOT A FACTOR
Must be done now	Should be done soon	Long-Range	Very Long-Range
1	2	3	4

C. DELEGATION

MUST BE DONE BY ME	CAN BE DELEGATED	CAN BE DELEGATED
I am only person who can do it	TO (A)	TO (B)
1	2	3

D. VISITATIONS AND CONFERENCES

PEOPLE I MUST SEE EACH DAY	PEOPLE TO SEE FREQUENTLY: Not Daily	PEOPLE TO SEE REGULARLY: Not Frequently	PEOPLE TO SEE ONLY INFRE- QUENTLY
1	2	3	4

DECISION MAKING AND CREATIVE PROBLEM SOLVING

Decision Making Versus Creative Problem Solving

There is a minor distinction between decision making and problem solving. Decision making involves the selection of a course of action from among known alternatives to accomplish an objective. Decision making occurs as a reaction to a problem and usually involves *programmed* decisions to the extent that they are repetitive, routine, frequent, and that a definite procedure is available for handling them. Problem solving also involves the selection of a course of action from alternatives to produce a desired result, but the decision is usually *nonprogrammed* in nature because there are unstructured, novel, and involve much uncertainty regarding cause and effect relationships AND require considerable **creativity** in generating possible solutions, since it has not arisen in exactly the same manner before or because of its extreme complexity or importance. Of course, most organizations and managers will face greater numbers of programmed decisions and they should not involve expending unnecessary organizational resources on them. On the other hand, the nonprogrammed problem solving process can involve much creativity and billions of dollars worth of resources. Unfortunately, modern management techniques have not made nearly the advances in improving nonprogrammed, creative problem solving, as they have in programmed decision making. Top managers deal primarily with nonprogrammed problem solving, while supervisors deal primarily with programmed decisions. So, the difference is in the types of decisions made, rather than the orderly process and procedure that is followed. The same process is used for decision making and for problem solving.

The assumptions of the decision making model are that the decision maker can be fully logical and objective, has a clear objective stated, and that the process will lead toward the selection of the alternative that will maximize the objective. So there is no conflict over the stated objective, all viable options and relevant criteria are identified, the criteria and alternatives can be mathematically ranked in a preferential order, the decision criteria and weights assigned to them are constant, and that the decision maker is rational. Most of these same assumptions apply to the problem solving model, except that all options and criteria, and their preferences and weights, may not be identified.

EXHIBIT # 16

The Decision Making-Problem Solving Process

Overview

Decisions should be thought of as means rather than the ends, since they are the organizational mechanisms through which an attempt is made to achieve a result. Every decision is the outcome of a dynamic process which is influenced by a multitude of variables. While the steps of the decision making and problem solving process are presented in an orderly, steplike system, this should not be interpreted to mean that it is a fixed and simple process. While selecting the optimal alternative course of action is the ultimate purpose of the process, some believe the initial problem definition step is the most important step. For example, the Kepner-Tregoe method of problem solving teaches that recognizing the problem is most important. Getting a good definition of the real problem is critical for making an intelligent and valid decision about a solution, or else the wrong problem will be solved. This method recognizes that one should define what the problem is not (as well as what it is), that the problem should be prioritized with other problems, and that there should be searching for cause and effect relationships.

The Process

The author's decision making-problem solving process follows:

THE DECISION MAKING - PROBLEM SOLVING PROCESS

1. SUMMARIZE THE *BACKGROUND* OF THE SITUATION

    Separate known facts from opinions; State ASSUMPTIONS; Distinguish emotions & feelings from objective data

2. ESTABLISH *OBJECTIVES*

    Determine results desired
    SPECIFICALLY state what you want to accomplish
    Ensure objectives are in quantifiable terms

3. DEFINE THE KEY *PROBLEM*

    State the major problem; then list related sub problems
    Succinctly and briefly say aloud "The major problem is... "
    Separate SYMPTOMS from the genuine issue
    Keep asking yourself "why" does this exist... to delimit the problem

4. GENERATE *ALTERNATIVE SOLUTIONS*... COURSES OF ACTION

    BRAINSTORM all possible solutions, no matter how ridiculous at first
    List at least 3 alternatives for each problem or sub-problem

5. *EVALUATE* ALTERNATIVE SOLUTIONS AGAINST OBJECTIVES & CRITERIA

Review initially-stated objectives
List major criteria for evaluation of solutions
Consider the pros and cons of EACH alternative separately
Test each alternative against each objective and criteria
Try to generate at least 3 pros and 3 cons for each alternative
Consider future consequences of each solution

6. *SELECT* THE BEST ALTERNATIVE SOLUTION

Choose the optimal solution based on analysis and subjective & objective criteria

7. DEVELOP AN *ACTION PLAN*

Implement the best solution... make it happen
Plan for short, intermediate, and long-run actions for implementation
Who, What, Where, When, and How actions
Follow-up for adjustments with milestone checks

Selected Tools and Techniques

Brainstorming

An idea-generating process that specifically encourages all possible alternatives to a decision or problem, while withholding any judgment or criticism of any alternative, is called brainstorming. In a typical session, several people sit around a table and the leader states the problem very clearly and ensures it is understood by all. Members then free-wheel and generate as many alternatives as possible in a given length of time. No criticism is allowed and all alternatives are recorded for later discussion and analysis. This process encourages the team members to be very creative, think the unusual, and let one idea stimulate another. Later there are discussions of each alternative. There is no attempt to arrive at a preferred solution during the brainstorming process.

Cause and effect Diagrams

Problem diagnosis attempts to identify the causes of the defined problem and a common tendency is to mistake symptoms for causes. The cause and effect diagram or "fishbone" diagram is a tool that can be used to separate causes from symptoms. It is called a fishbone diagram because it resembles the skeleton of a fish. According to Kaoru Ishikawa, it pictorially illustrates the relationship among a certain outcome and all the factors that influence the outcome. The problem or objective is placed in a box on the diagram with a straight problem line shown. Major categories of influencing factors are shown as branch arrows to the main problem line on the diagram. Commonly used categories are manpower, materials, methods, machines (4Ms). Subfactors are shown as branch arrows to the major factors lines. All factors having an effect, both significant and casual, are shown on the diagram. After team discussion and prioritizing factors, issues are debated and analyzed to differentiate major from minor causes, to reveal relationships between causes, and to arrive at the root cause of the problem.

Pareto Analysis

Pareto Analysis allows data to be considered according to priority and importance. Pareto charts are bar charts which depict problem categories and their frequencies of occurrence. After problems are identified, existing problem data is grouped by comparable units of measurement. Problem categories are shown as bars on the horizontal axis and frequencies of occurrence are shown on the left vertical axis. The categories are ordered according to their frequencies and shown by bars for visual comparison purposes.

Nominal Group Technique

The Nominal Group Technique is another useful process for helping organizational groups to make decisions. This process is designed to ensure that each group member has equal participation in making the group decision. It involves the following steps:

STEP #1: Each group member writes down individual ideas on the decision or problem being discussed.

STEP #2: Each member presents individual ideas orally. The ideas are usually written on a board or large sheet of paper for all other members to see and refer to.

STEP #3: After all members present their ideas, the entire group discusses the ideas simultaneously. Discussion tends to be unstructured and spontaneous.

STEP #4: When discussion is completed, a secret ballot is taken to allow members to support their favorite ideas without fear of intimidation. The idea receiving the most votes is adopted and implemented.

Delphi Technique

The Delphi Technique is still another useful process for helping groups to make decisions. This technique involves circulating questionnaires on a specific problem among group members, sharing the questionnaire results with them, and then continuing to recirculate and refine individual responses until a consensus regarding the problem is reached. In contrast to the Nominal Group Technique or brainstorming, the Delphi Technique does not have group members meet face-to-face. The formal steps in the Delphi Technique are:

STEP #1: A problem is identified and specifically defined.

STEP #2: Group members are asked to offer solutions to the problem by providing anonymous responses to a carefully-designed questionnaire.

STEP #3: Responses of all group members are compiled and sent out to all group members.

STEP #4: Individual group members are asked to generate a new individual solution to the problem after they have studied and reflected on the individual responses of all other group members compiled in Step # 3.

STEP #5: Steps #3 and #4 are repeated until a consensus problem solution is reached.

Other Techniques

Cost-Benefit Analysis:

The supervisor can use *cost-benefit analysis* to compare the costs and benefits associated with a particular alternative course of action. The supervisor must gather data on not only the financial expenses of an alternative, but also other costs for choosing it, e.g. the personnel labor costs of adding people to the project, equipment expenses, administrative costs, the costs of selecting one vendor over another, and the costs of foregoing another alternative or expected opportunity loss costs. These total costs are then compared against the potential payoffs and benefits of pursuing the action.

Marginal Analysis:

Marginal analysis, or incremental analysis, helps decision makers optimize returns or minimize costs. It can be used to determine the extra output that can be attained by adding an extra unit of input. The profit maximization rule is utilized to get output to the point where marginal revenue exceeds marginal costs or are at least equals it. It does not deal with the "average" cost, but rather the "additional" revenue that would be generated by a particular action and what "additional" costs would result.

Myers-Briggs Type Indicator:

The *Myers-Briggs Type Indicator* (MBI) is a 126-item survey that helps identify an individual's problem-solving type. While it measures eight dimensions of types of decision making, we shall focus on the four internal dimensions which are:

(1) **SENSING**... versus

(2) **INTUITION**...and

(3) **THINKING**... versus

(4) **FEELING**

They are directly related to decision making and problem solving. While everyone uses all four dimensions, each of us tends to develop and use one information-gathering dimension and one information-evaluating dimension more than the others. The ideal is to maintain a balance by developing capability in all four dimensions. Although experience and growth opportunities can help develop weaker dimensions, most people have developed two of the dimensions more than the others. Two of the functions have much greater influence in the development of perception and making judgments.

There are two ways of perceiving: **sensing** (becoming aware of things through the five senses) and **intuition** (the ability to know things without the use of rational thinking processes). The MBI says people develop a preference for one or the other. Those who rely on sensing tend to be patient, practical, and realistic, while those who rely on intuition tend to be impatient, creative, and idea and theory oriented.

There are also two ways of deciding: **thinking** (using a logical process of rational reasoning) and **feeling** (using innate processes that include values and beliefs in arriving at conclusions). People with a feeling orientation tend to be humanistic, sympathetic, and subjective in decision making, while thinking types use logic, objectivity, and careful examination of facts.

The four combinations of sensing-thinking, intuitive-thinking, sensing-feeling, and intuitive-feeling have a definite influence on problem solving and decision making. Ideally, a balance may be developed by using all four functions in decision making.

Program Evaluation and Review Technique (PERT):

The Program Evaluation and Review Technique (PERT) was developed in 1958 by the U.S. Navy for developing the Polaris Fleet Ballistic Missile and is credited generally with saving about two years on the project. PERT is a planning and control method for projects which graphically represents the project's steps and the timing and linkages among the steps. The projects can range from designing and introducing a new automobile to building a house to planning a wedding, but usually PERT is reserved for products with thousands of events and activities. Events and activities are the two major components of PERT networks. Events (network circles) represent specific accomplishments or performance milestones, while activities (network arrows) are the time-consuming aspects of the project which represent the work needed to complete a particular event. An event does not consume time nor resources. By studying the PERT chart, the planner can determine the "critical path" which is the sequence of critical events that in total requires the most time to complete. Planners can identify bottlenecks and potential trouble spots, compare different methods for reaching the project goal, devote attention to critical tasks, and identify a realistic time for completion of the project. He can then make modifications in activities as necessary to help accomplish the project.

Breakeven Analysis:

Breakeven Analysis is a financial decision-making tool that enables a manager to determine whether a particular volume of sales will result in losses or profits. It uses four basic concepts: fixed costs, variable costs, revenues, and profits. A breakeven chart is used to graphically show whether a particular volume of sales will result in profit or losses. The breakeven point is the point where the total revenues equal total costs. Beyond that point an organization can expect to earn a profit and below this point it can expect a loss. Both a chart and a formula can be used to determine breakeven points.

The Breakeven Formula:

$P(X) = F + V(X)$ where

F = fixed costs

V = variable costs per unit

X = volume of output (in units)

P = price per unit

CONCEPTS AND STRATEGIES OF SCIENTIFIC PROBLEM SOLVING

Incomplete Information Concept

Even if managers did have an unlimited ability to evaluate information, they still would not be able to arrive at the optimum decision because they would have incomplete information. Information is incomplete because the full range of decision-making alternatives is unknowable in most situations and the consequences associated with know alternatives are uncertain. In essence, information is incomplete because of risk and uncertainty, ambiguity, and time constraints.

Satisficing Concept

Faced with *"bounded rationality"* (or the cognitive limitations that constrain one's ability and paradigms to interpret, process, and act on information) and the high information costs and time limitations, most managers do not attempt to discover every, or even a high number of alternatives to solve their problem. Instead, managers use a strategy known as *"satisficing"* or exploring a limited sample of all potential alternatives. According to March and Simon in their 1958 book Organizations, when managers satisfice, they search for and choose acceptable, or satisfactory ways to respond to problems and opportunities rather than trying to make the best possible decision. Since managerial decision making is often more art than science, managers must rely on their intuition and judgment to make what seems to them to be the best decision in the face of uncertainty and ambiguity. By satisficing, managers make an acceptable decision, but just not the very best decision, thus freeing up resources and efforts to allow other departments or segments of the total organization to reach goals instrumental for the success of the whole system.

Strategies of Scientific Problem Solving

- Collect Meaningful Data-- Clarify operational definitions, so everyone will take measurements in the same way

- Identify Root Causes of Problems-- Do not react to symptoms, ask what really caused this; do not zero-in on one cause too early; explore many potential sources of problems

- Develop Appropriate Solutions-- Open-up your thinking; do not assume you know the cause of the problem before starting; support hunches with data

- Plan and Make Changes—Do not ready, fire, aim; ready, aim, fire... PLAN; do not act just for action, but if it is the right thing to do; work one process at a time

Suboptimization

Suboptimization is a condition where subobjectives are conflicting or not directly aimed at accomplishing the overall organizational objectives. It is possible within an organization when one subobjective exists for a department which is in conflict with another department's subobjective. For example, an operational department desires funds over-and-above their budgeted funds for a new computer system to better serve a particular client's needs, but the accounting department will not approve release of additional capital equipment funds for the purchase because of their subobjective of maintaining budgeted expenses. When their are competing subobjectives, a manager would have to choose which subobjective would better contribute to obtaining overall **ORGANIZATIONAL** objectives and take precedence. Since controlling suboptimization is a normal part of a manager's responsibilities, managers must develop a thorough understanding of the overall organization's mission, vision, goals, and objectives and how various departments and divisions of the organization relate to one another to ensure that subobjectives properly reflect these relations.

Suggested Problem Solving and Decision Making Guidelines

Guidelines

Some suggested decision making and problem solving guidelines are:

1). **Differentiate Between Big Decisions and Little Problems.** Decide which major problems and big decisions should be dealt with and what little problems and decisions can be dealt with later. The big problems are going to require more creativity and time and this must be planned for.
2). **Rely on Established Policy When Possible.** Use established policies and procedures as guides for action in routine decision making.
3). **Consult With Others.** Other well-informed supervisors, specialists, and resource people can be sought for useful insight and data, but not to make the decision for you.
4). **Avoid Crisis Decisions.** Deciding under stress is not an ideal situation. Take time out to reflect and make the decision later when possible. Some crisis decisions can be avoided by anticipating problems and by avoiding procrastination.
5). **Forget All Eventualities.** Do not try to spend time thinking about everything that can go wrong and letting negativity set in. Be positive and stick to the highly probable outcomes.
6). **Admit Mistakes.** There will be good AND bad decisions made. Recognize when a decision is less than satisfactory, but do not let it bog you down. Instead roll with the punches, learn from the situation, and have self-confidence to make better decisions.
7). **Be Decisive.** Indecision creates tensions in supervisors and they may lose the respect of others. When all the data and inputs are there for a decision, make it. When more data is available, a new and different decision can be made.
8). **Implement.** Once a decision is made, make it happen. Effective leadership is necessary to follow through, communicate the decision to workers, and motivate them to implement it. Poor implementation can ruin a great decision.

Group Behaviors

Two group behaviors have the potential to affect a team's ability to objectively appraise alternative actions and to determine a quality solution in decision making and problem solving: group pressure and group exaggeration. **Group pressures** for conformity can deter a group from critically appraising unusual, minority, or unpopular views. It can drastically hinder a group's performance. The second behavior is **group exaggeration**. This occurs when a group is discussing a given set of alternatives to arrive at a solution and the members tend to exaggerate the initial position they hold to convince the group into accepting it. The first behavior, group pressure, can stop members from speaking up in formal meetings and in informal groups, when they become so enamored with fitting in and seeking concurrence that the norm for consensus overrides the realistic appraisal of alternative courses of action and the complete expression of the unpopular view. Group members rationalize any resistance to the assumptions they have made. No matter how strongly the evidence may contradict their assumptions, they behave as to reinforce their assumptions. They apply direct pressure on those who express doubts and there appears to be an illusion of unanimity. We generally find it more pleasant to be in agreement than to be a disruptive force and do not voice the opinion which could improve the effectiveness of the decision. The second behavior, group exaggeration, occurs when the group discussion leads to a significant shift in the direction toward which they were already leaning before the discussion. Conservative types become more cautious and the aggressive types become more aggressive and take on more risk. The group discussion tends to exaggerate the initial position of the group. What are the practical applications of these two behaviors? Supervisors must realize that group pressures will be applied and that group decisions exaggerate the initial position of the individual members, so a more optimal decision can be made considering these variables.

Ethical Considerations

Definitions:

Ethics are the fundamental principles and standards of conduct governing an individual, group, or organization. Ethical considerations and decisions always involve normative judgments where the manager or worker must place a value judgment or assess if something is good or bad, right or wrong, pro or con, or better or worse. These ethical considerations and decisions always involve a society's or group's or organization's acceptable norms of behavior or *moral standards*.

Characteristics of Moral Standards:

Moral Standards:

1). **Address matters of serious consequence** to all individuals within organizations. There are personal moral standards against lying, slander, defaming, stealing, cheating, murder, rape, and price-fixing because there is a large majority consensus that such actions pose a serious threat to the well-being of society, organizations, and individuals.

2). **Cannot be changed or established by directive decisions** and procedures of authoritative bodies like boards, councils, or legislatures. Moral standards are particular individual issues and decisions that transcend the prescribed actions of organizations and groups.

3). **Should override and take priority over self-interest.** For example, if you have a moral obligation to do something, you are expected to do it even if doing so might impede your career, cost you money, or cause you to loose an association or relationship with someone. The big picture, total system, society, or human race perspective takes priority over one person's self-interest and subsystem.

4). **Are never situational.** What is morally right (or wrong) in one situation is always right (or wrong) in another situation. For example, the fact that the organization will benefit if a manager makes a hiring decision based on a biased priority to a personal friend, does not make the biased priority in hiring right.

5). **Tend to generate strong emotions.** For example, violating moral standards may make you feel ashamed, embarrassed, or remorseful. Likewise, if you observe someone else acting immorally, you may feel angry, offended, indignant and resentful.

Managers should note that the law itself is not an adequate guide or explanation for whether or not a decision or action is ethical. A decision or action can be legal, but not ethical and the reverse is also true. For example, a decision (involving ethics) can be made to terminate someone's employment with an organization strictly based on what is legal, but that does not guarantee that the decision will be ethical nor support ethical considerations. Specifically, a manager making a decision to release the worker just a few months before he is vested in the organization's pension plan may be unethical, but not illegal.

Fostering Work Ethics

A 1993 study by Ron Zemke concluded that fostering ethics at work involves the following five steps:

Step#1: Emphasize Top Management's Commitment. The chief executive officer and top managers need to be strongly and openly committed to ethical behavior and conduct in all their actions and decisions. Their leadership in defining, focusing on, and showing strong support for the values of the organization are very key factors in implementing ethics in the workplace.

Step#2: Prepare and Publish a Code of Ethical Conduct. The entire organization must be aware of and have access to written principles of conduct and expected standards of behavior . For example, a code could include statements about fundamental honesty, adherence to laws, and professional respect for other Board members.

Step#3: Establish compliance measures. Practical applications and policies and procedures should be in place to inform, educate, motivate, and remind all workers of the priority of practicing ethical behavior and reporting unethical behavior. For example, instituting communication programs to inform and motivate workers about expected ethical behavior and a procedure specifying penalties for violations.

Step#4: Involve Personnel at All Levels.

BIBLIOGRAPHY

Alderfer, C.P. *Existence, Relatedness, and Growth: Human Needs in Organizational Settings.* New York: Free Press, 1972.

Allport, G.W. *Personality: A Psychological Interpretation.* New York: Holt, Rinehart & Winston, 1937.

Argyris, Chris. *Organization and Innovation.* Homewood, Ill.: Dorsey Press and R.D. Irwin, 1965.

Argyris, Chris. *Reasoning, Learning, and Action: Individual & Organizational.* San Francisco: Jossey-Bass, 1982.

Bass, Bernard M. "From Transactional to Transformational Leadership: Learning to Share the Vision," *Organizational Dynamics,* 18 (Winter 1990), 19-31.

Bass, Bernard M., and B. Avolio, "Developing Transformational Leadership: 1992 and Beyond," *Journal of European Industrial Training,* January 1990, 23.

Bass, Bernard M., and Ralph M. Stogdill. *Stogdill's Handbook of Leadership* (3rd ed.) New York: Free Press, 1990.

Batten, Joe D. *Tough-Minded Leadership.* New York: American Management Association, 1989.

Bennis, Warren. "Managing the Dream: Leadership in the 21st. Century," *Training,* 27 (May 1990), 43-46.

Bennis, Warren. *On Becoming a Leader.* Reading, Mass.: Addison-Wesley, 1989.

Bennis, Warren. *Organization Development: Its Nature, Origins, and Prospects.* Reading, MA.: Addison-Wesley, 1969.

Blake, Robert and Jane Mouton. *The Managerial Grid III.* Houston, TX.: Gulf Publishing Company, 1984.

Bramson, R.M. *Coping With Difficult People.* New York: Doubleday, 1981.

Burns, J.M. *Leadership.* New York: Harper & Row, 1978.

Cherrington, D. and S. Condie, and J. England, "Age and Work Values," *Academy of Management Journal,* September 1979, 617-623.

Covey, S.R. *Principle Centered Leadership.* New York: Summit Books, 1991.

Covey, S.R. *The Seven Habits of Highly Effective People.* New York: Simon and Schuster, 1989.

Crosby, Phillip B. *Leading: The Art of Becoming an Executive.* New York: McGraw-Hill, 1990.

Davis, Keith. "Management Communication and the Grapevine," *Harvard Business Review,* January/February 1953, 43-49.

Deming, W.E. *Out of the Crisis.* Cambridge, MA.: MIT, Center for Advanced Engineering Studies, 1990.

Dessler, Gary. *Human Resources Management,* 7th ed., Upper Saddle River, N.J.: Prentice Hall, 1997.

Drucker, Peter F. *Managing for Results.* New York: Harper & Row, 1986.

Drucker, Peter F. *Managing the Future.* New York: Dutton, 1992.

Drucker, Peter F. *The New Realities: In Government and Politics-In Economics and Business-In Society and World Views.* New York: Harper & Row, 1990.

Drucker, Peter F. *The Practice of Management.* New York: Harper & Row, 1986.

Fayol, Henri. *Industrial and General Administration.* Paris: Dunod, 1925.

Fiedler, Fred E. *A Theory of Leadership Effectiveness.* New York: McGraw-Hill, 1967.

Fiedler, Fred E., and Martin M. Chemers. *Improving Leadership Effectiveness: The Leader Match Concept* (2nd ed.). Wiley Press, 1984.

Findley, Benjamin F. Jr. "Cyberspace Law and the Rights of Internet Users in Higher Education," *Higher Education Law Journal,* Vol VI, No.1, Spring, 1997, San Diego, CA: College and University Law Press, 1997.

Findley, Benjamin F. Jr. *Job Application, Interviewing, and Resume' Preparation* (2nd ed.). Findley Management Consulting, Inc., 1986.

Findley, Benjamin F. Jr., and Frank L. Goldstein. *Leadership and Airpower Issues for the Twenty-First Century.* Montgomery: Air University Press, U.S. Air Force, 1997.

Findley, Benjamin F. Jr. *Principles of Supervision, CD-ROM,* Montgomery: U.S Air Force, ECI, Gunter AFB, AL, 1998.

Findley, Benjamin F. Jr. "Time Management: A Systematic Approach," *Practical Supervision Journal*, Austin, TX: Practical Supervision, Inc., 1985.

Gardner, John W. "The Moral Aspects of Leadership," *NAASP Bulletin*, 73 (January 1989), 43.

Gellerman, Saul W. *Management by Motivation.* New York: American Management Association, 1968.

Ghiselli, Edwin E. *Measurement Theory for the Behavior Sciences.* New York: W. H. Freeman & Company, 1981.

Goldstein, Frank L., and Benjamin F. Findley, Jr. *Psychological Operations.* Montgomery: Air University Press, U.S. Air Force, 1996.

Graicunas, A. V. "Relationships in Organizations," in *Papers On The Science of Administration*, L. Gulick and L. Urwick (eds.) New York: Columbus University Press, 1947, 183-187.

Guest, Robert H., et al. *Organizational Change Through Effective Leadership* (2nd ed.). Englewood Cliffs, N.J.: Prentice Hall, 1986.

Guest, Robert, Paul Hersey, and Kenneth Blanchard. *Organizational Change Through Effective Leadership.* Englewood Cliffs, N.J.: Prentice Hall, 1977.

Harris, O.J. *Managing People At Work.* New York: John Wiley & Sons, 1976.

Harris, T.W. "Listen Carefully," *Nation's Business*, 77 (1989), 78.

Hackman, J. R., and G. R. Oldham. *Work Design.* Reading, Mass.: Addison-Wesley, 1980.

Hersey, Paul. *The Situational Leader.* Escondido, Calif.: Center for Leadership Studies, 1984.

Hersey, Paul, and Kenneth H. Blanchard. "Life Cycle Theory of Leadership," *Training and Development Journal*, 23 (May 1969).

Herzberg, Frederick. "One More Time: How Do You Motivate Employees?" *Harvard Business Review*, 65 (September-October 1987), 109-21.

Herzberg, Frederick. *Work and the Nature of Man*. New York: World Publishing Co., 1966.

Hodgetts, Richard. *Effective Supervision*. New York: McGraw-Hill, 1987.

House, Robert J. :A Path-Goal Theory of Leader Effectiveness," *Administrative Science Quarterly*, 23 (1978), 496-504.

House, Robert J., and Terrence Mitchell. :Path-Goal Theory of Leadership," *Journal of Contemporary Business*, Autumn 1974, 81-98.

Juran, J. *Juran on Quality by Design*. New York: The Free Press, 1992.

Kepner, C.H. and B.B. Tregoe *The Rational Manager*. New York: Princeton Research Press, 1976.

Kiechel, W. "How To Take Part in a Meeting," *Fortune* (May 26, 1986): 177-180.

Korda, Michael. *Power! How To Get It, How To Use It* . New York: Ballantine Books, 1976.

Lawler, E. E. *High Involvement Management*. San Francisco: Jossey-Bass, 1990.

Lewin, K. *Field Theory in Social Science*. New York: Harper & Row, 1951.

Lewin, K., R. Lippett, and R. White. "Leader Behavior and Member Reaction in Three Social Climates," in *Group Dynamics: Research and Theory* (2nd ed.), eds. D. Cartwright and A. Zander. Evanston, Ill.: Row, Peterson & Co., 1960.

Likert, Rensis. *Human Organization: Its Management and Values*. New York: McGraw-Hill, 1967.

Locke, E., E. Frederick, C. Lee, and P. Bobko, "Effect of Self-Efficacy, Goals, and Task Strategies on Task Performance," *Journal of Applied Psychology*, May 1984, 241-51.

Luft, Joseph and Harry Ingham, "The Johari Window, A Graphic Model of Interpersonal Awareness," *Proceedings of the Western Training Laboratory in Group Development*. Los Angeles: UCLA Extension Office, 1955.

March, J.G. and H. Simon. *Organizations*. New York: Wiley, 1958.
Margerison, A. and D. McCann. *Team Management: Practical New Approaches*. London: Mercury Books, 1990.
Maslow, Abraham H. *Motivation and Personality*. New York: Harper & Row, 1954.
Mayo, Elton. *The Human Problems of an Industrial Civilization*. Boston: Harvard Business School, 1977.
McClelland, David C. *The Achieving Society*. Princeton, N. J.: D. Van Norstrand Co., Inc., 1967.
McClelland, David C. *The Achievement Motive*. New York: Appleton-Century-Crofts, 1953.
McConkey, Dale. *No Nonsense Delegation*. New York: AMACOM, a division of American Management Association, 1974, 154.
McGregor, Douglas. *The Human Side of Enterprise* (35th Anniversary ed.). New York: McGraw-Hill, 1985.
Mehrabian, Albert. *Silent Messages*. Belmont, CA: Wadsworth, 1971.
Mintzberg, H. *The Nature of Managerial Work*. New York: Harper & Row, 1973.
Naisbitt, John. *Megatrends*. New York: Warner Books, 1982.
Odiorne, George S. *Management Decisions by Objectives*. New York: Pitman Publishing Corp., 1968.
Ouchi, W.G. *Theory Z: How American Business Can Meet the Japanese Challenge*. Reading, MA.: Addison-Wesley, 1981.
Peters, Thomas J., and Robert Waterman. *In Search of Excellence*. New York: Harper & Row, 1982.
Robbins, Stephen P. *Organizational Behavior: Concepts, Controversies, and Applications*, 4th ed., Englewood Cliffs, N.J.: Prentice Hall, 1989.
Roberts, K. and C. Roberts, "Failures in Upward Communication in Organizations," *Academy of Management Journal,* 17, no.2 (June 1974), 205-215.
Rogers, Carl. *On Becoming A Person*. Boston: Houghton-Mifflin Company, 1961.
Schein, Edgar. *Organizational Culture and Leadership, 2nd ed.,*. San Francisco: Jossey-Bass, 1992.

Seltz, D. and Alfred Modica. *Negotiate Your Way To Success*. Rockville Centre, NY: Farnsworth, 1980.

Senge, Peter M. *The Fifth Discipline: The Art & Practice of the Learning Organization*. New York: Doubleday, 1990.

Senge, Peter M. "The Leaders New Work: Building Learning Organizations," *Sloan Management Review*, 32 (Fall 1990), 7-19.

Simon, Herbert A. *Administrative Behavior* New York: Free Press, 1976.

Skinner, B.F. *Analysis of Behavior*. New York: McGraw-Hill, 1961.

Smith, Perry M. "Twenty Guidelines for Leadership, " *Nation's Business*, 77 (September 1989), 60-61.

Stogdill, Ralph M. *Handbook of Leadership*. New York: The Free Press, 1974.

Stogdill, Ralph M. , and Alvin E. Coons, eds. *Leader Behavior: Its Description and Measurement, Research Monograph No. 88.* Columbus: Bureau of Business Research, The Ohio State University, 1957.

Tannenbaum, Robert, and Warren Schmidt. "How to Choose a Leadership Pattern," *Harvard Business Review,* March-April, 1958. 95-102.

Taylor, Frederick W. *The Principles of Scientific Management*. New York: Harper & Brothers, 1991.

Toffler, A. *Powershift: Knowledge, Wealth and Violence at the Edge of the 21st Century*. London: Bantam, 1990.

U.S. Department of the Air Force. *United States Air Force Core Values*. Washington, D.C.: Government Printing Office, 1997.

Vroom, Victor H., and Arthur Jago. *The New Leadership: Managing Participation in Organizations*. Englewood Cliffs, N.J.: Prentice Hall, 1988.

Walton, Mary. *The Deming Management Method*. New York: Perigee Books, The Putnam Publishing Group, 1986.

Whyte, W. F., ed. *Money and Motivation*. New York: Harper & Row, Pub., 1955.

Zaleznik, Abraham. "The Leadership Gap," *Academy of Management Executive*, 4 (February 1990), 7-22.

INDEX

A

Acceptance, Delegation, 92
Adaptability Principle, 9
Administrative-Conceptual Skills, 9
Air Force Values Model, 101
Alderfer's ERG Model, 113
Allocation, of Time, 145
Allport's Values, 99
Analysis, SWOT, 85
Answers, Time Use Quiz, 142
Assertive Behavior, 29
Assessing, Job's Motivating Potential, 121
Assessment, Needs Exercise, 108
Assumptions, and Facts, Attitudes, 147
Assumptions, and Limitations, 88, 147
Attitude, 88, 96, 122, 147
Attitudes, and Job Satisfaction, 96
Authority Process, 88

B

Barriers, Common, Communication, 54
Barriers, Common, Delegation, 92
Barriers in Dealing With Diversity, 16
Bases for Diversity, 15
Basic Counseling Function, 42
Basic Planning & Time Management, 141
Basic Principles, Skills, and Behaviors, Management, 5
Behaviors, Assertive, 29
Behaviors, Group, 27, 173
Behavior, Internal vs. External Influences, 95

Behavior, Leader Models, 127
Behaviors, Self-Oriented, 27, 95
Behavior Modification, 98
Benchmarking, 5
Benefit, Cost Analysis, 165
Blake and Mouton's Managerial Grid, 127
Blanchard, Hersey Life Cycle Model, 134, 137
Blending Behavior, Values, Needs, and Motivation, 122
Brainstorming, 163
Breakeven Point Analysis, 168

C

Cause & Effect Diagram, 163
Change, Organizational & Individual Perspectives, 30
Change, Responses, 31
Change, Strategies, 31
Change Process, 30
Channels, Formal and Informal, Communication, 56
Characteristics, Effective Followers, 126
Characteristics, High-Performing Team, 19
Characteristics, Organizational Development, 34
Characteristics, Transformational Leadership, 138
Characteristics of Moral Standards, 174
Characteristics of Practical Objectives, 82
Clarification, Performance Standards, 40
Coaching, Role for Managers, 36
Cohesiveness, Group, 20
Collaboration Skills, 47
Common Barriers, Communication, 54
Common Barriers, Delegation, 92
Communication, Effective, Guidelines, 66
Communication, Logical Reasoning Fallacies, 59
Communication, Oral and Written, 56
Communication, Technological Factors, 70

Communication Process, 52
Computer Crime, 72
Concept, Incomplete Information, 169
Concept, Motivation, 94
Concept, Organizational Politics, 21
Concept, Satisficing, 169
Concept, Transformational Leadership, 138
Concepts, Scientific Problem Solving, 169
Concepts, Time Management, 145
Conceptual, Administrative Skill, 9, 13
Conclusions, Motivation, 123
Conclusions, Needs, 114
Conflict Resolution, 43
Conflict Resolution, Styles, 44
Consensus Concept, 25
Consensus Definition, 25
Consensus and Win-Win, 51
Considerations, Ethical, 174
Considerations for Planning and Setting Objectives, 84
Considerations in Successful Delegation, 90
Constructive Confrontation, 37
Contingency, Fiedler's Model, 132
Controlling, 3, 141
Controlling, Managing Time, 141
Coordinating, 4
Core Values Model, 101
Cost-Benefit Analysis, 165
Counseling, Role for Managers, 39
Counseling, Worker Guidelines, 42
Counseling vs. Disciplinary Action, 41
Criteria for Verifiable Objectives, 82
Cultural Variables, Leadership, 125
Cyberspace Law Considerations, 72
Cyberstalking, 76

D

Dealing, Opposition to Ideas, 44
Dealing, Specific Problem People, 48
Decision Making, Overview, 160
Decision Making, Process, 160, 161
Decision Making, Versus Creative Problem Solving, 159
Decision Making Tools And Techniques, 163
Delegation, Checklist for Effective, 93
Delegation, Philosophy and Attitude, 88
Delegation, Process, 89
Delegation, Steps, 89
Delphi Technique, 165
Deming's Total Quality Management System, 107
Develop, Listening Skills, 63
Development, Organizational, 34
Differences, Status, 59
Directing, 3
Disciplinary, Action, 41
Diversity, 15
Diversity, Barriers, 16
Diversity, Bases, 15
Dominant Values, Work Force, 100

E

Effective Communication Guidelines, 66
Effective Delegation, Checklist, 93
Effective Delegation, Obstacles, 92
Effective Followers, 126
Effective Group Criteria, 10
Electronic Mail, 74
Elements, Communication Process, 52
Elements of Effectiveness, Findley's, 10
Employee Involvement, Empowerment, 14, 86
Empowerment, Self-Managed Teams, 14

Equal Employment Opportunity Legislation, 34
Ethical Considerations, 174
Exception, Management, Principle, 8
Expectancies Models, 118

F

Fallacies, Logical Reasoning, 59
Fayol's Principles, 5
Feedback, Communication, 53
Feedback, Delegation, 91
Feedback, and Follow-up Communication, 65
Fiedler's Contingency Model, 132
Findley's Effectiveness Elements, 11
Focus on Issues, Not Blame, 38
Focus on Mutual Benefits, Not Win-Lose, 38
Follower's, Effective, 126
Formal and Informal Channels, 56
Fostering Work Ethics, 176
Functions, Managerial, 3

G

General Time Saving Techniques, 156
Goals, Objectives and Priorities, 86, 148
Goals Versus Objectives, 80
Grapevine, 56
Group Behaviors, 27, 173
Group Cohesiveness, 20
Group Criteria, 10
Group Development, 18
Group Dynamics, 10
Guidelines, Positive Climate, 26, 122
Guidelines, Problem Solving, 172
Guidelines, Top 10 Time Management, 149

H

Hackman and Oldham's Job Characteristics Model, 120
Hawthorne Effect, 97
Hersey-Blanchard Life Cycle Model, 134, 137
Herzberg's Motivators and Hygienes, 116
Hidden Agendas, 37
High-Performing Team, Characteristics, 19
Hints, Conflict Resolution, 47
House's Path-Goal Model, 133
Human Skills, 9, 12

I

Importance of Planning, 78
Importance and Time Allocation, 145
Incentives, Delegation, 91
Incomplete Information Concept, 169
Increasing Power, Strategies, 22
Informal, Formal Channels, 56
Integrating Motivational Concepts, 122
Internal Versus External Influences on Behavior, 95
Internet, 70
Interpersonal Conflict Resolution, 44
Inventory of Personal Utilization, 141
Involvement, Employee, 86

J

Job Characteristics Model, 120
Job Satisfaction, 96
Job's Motivating Potential, 121
Johari Window, Communication, 70

K

Key Considerations in Delegation, 90
Key Equal Employment Opportunity Legislation, 34
Key Negotiation Strategies, 68

L

Leader Behavior Models, 127
Leadership, Transformational, 138
Leadership Conclusions, 139
Leadership Issues, 125
Learning Organization, 32
Likert, University of Michigan Studies, Leadership, 130
Listening Skills, 63
Logical Reasoning Fallacies, Communication, 59

M

MBO Process, 81
McClelland's Three Needs, 114
McGregor's Theory X and Theory Y, 115
Management, Supervision, and Leadership Concepts, 1
Management, Time, 141
Management, Time Concepts, 145
Management, Time, Guidelines, 149
Management, Time, Philosophy, 147
Management Tools, Time, 148
Management By Exception Principle, 8
Managerial Functions and Roles, 3
Managing Change, 30
Managing Interruptions, 156
Marginal Analysis, 166
Maslow's Need Hierarchy, 112
Messages, Nonverbal, 62
Michigan Studies, 130

Mission and Vision, 84
Models, Leader Behavior, 127
Models, Trait, 127
Modification, Behavior, 98
Moral Standards, 174
Motivating Potential, Jobs, 120
Motivation, Conclusions, 122
Motivation Models, 115
Motivation Process, 94
Myers-Briggs Type Indicator, 166

N

Needs, Conclusions, 114
Needs Assessment Exercise, 108
Negotiation Strategies, 68
Nominal Group Technique, 164
Nonverbal Messages, 62

O

OD Characteristics, 34
OD Objectives, 33
Objective Difficulty, 90
Objective Specificity, 90
Objectives, Characteristics, 82
Objectives, Purposes, 81
Objectives, Setting, 84
Objectives, Verifiable Criteria, 82
Objectivity Principle, 9
Ohio State University Studies, 129
Openness & Trust Model, 70
Opposition to Ideas, 43
Oral and Written Communication, 56
Organizational Development (OD), 33

Organizational Politics, 18, 21
Organizing, 3
Overcoming Obstacles to Delegation, 92
Overview, Decision Making Process, 159

P

Pareto Analysis, 64
Path-Goal Model, Situational Leadership, 133
Perception, Selective, 58
Performance Counseling Concept, 39
Performance Standards, 40
Personal Time Utilization, 141
Planning, 3
Planning, Importance, 78
Planning Steps, 78
Planning and Time Management, 141
Politics, Organizational, 18, 21
Porter-Lawler Expectancy Model, 118
Positive Climate Guidelines, 122
Power Leadership, 22, 126
Power, Strategies, 22, 126
Practical Objectives, Characteristics, 82
Predicting Performance, 124
Principles, Fayol's, 5
Priorities, Planning, 85
Priority System, Work, 157
Problem People, Dealing With, 43, 48
Problem Solving Guidelines, 172
Problem Solving, Process, 160
Problems, Specific, Time Management, 150
Process, Change, 30
Process, Leadership, 125
Productivity and Satisfaction Relationship, 139
Program Evaluation and Review Technique (PERT), 167
Purpose, Communication Process, 52
Purpose, Objectives, 81

Q

Quality Management, Total (TQM), 107
Quiz, Time Use, 142

R

Resolution, Conflict, 43
Resolution Hints, 47
Responses To Change, 31
Restructuring, 14

S

SWOT Analysis, Planning, 85
Satisficing, 169
Selective Perception, 58
Self-Oriented Behaviors, 27, 28
Situational Considerations, Conflict Resolution, 46
Situational Models, Leadership, 130
Skills, Management, 5, 9
Specific Signs, Troubled Worker, 39
Stages of Group Development, 18
Status Differences, 59
Steps in Delegation Process, 89
Strategies, Change, 31
Strategies for Increasing Power, 22
Strategies for Successful Communication, 62
Strategies of Scientific Problem Solving, 169
Suboptimization, 170
Successful Organization's Values, 105
Supervision, 2
Synergy, 20

T

TQM, 106, 107
Tannenbaum and Schmidt's Continuum, Leadership, 128
Team Building, 10
Team Roles, 23
Teams, Self-Managed, 14
Technological Factors, Communication, 70
Time Delay Value, 38
Time Management, 141, 148
Time Management Concepts, 145
Time Management Philosophy, 147
Time Management Problems and Solutions, 150
Time Management Tools, 148
Time Use Quiz, 142
Trait Model, Leadership, 127
Transformational Leadership, 138
Troubled Worker, Signs, 39
Types of Teams, 27
Typical SWOT Questions, 86

U

Understand Nonverbal Messages, 62
Useful Conclusions, Motivation, 123
Useful Conclusions, Needs, 114
Utilize Feedback, 53, 65

V

Values, Allport's, 99
Values, Core, Model, 101
Values, Definition, 99
Values, Successful Organizations, 105
Values, Work Force, 100
Verifiable Objectives, 82

Vision Statement, 84
Vroom Expectancy Model, Motivation, 118

W

Win-Win, Consensus, 51
Work Ethics, 175
Work Priority System, 157
Worker Counseling, Guidelines, 42

Z

Theory Z, 116